Praise for *Anchored in Love*

John Carter Cash was born into royalty, the answer to his legendary parents' prayers. I can still see the picture—on the front page of the newspaper in Lima, Peru—of John and June's joyful faces beaming down at the tiny piece of their love made visible.

The apple didn't fall too far from the tree, both a blessing and a curse, and John Carter's life—like that of his parents—has been full of higher highs and lower lows than most. But his heart and his soul, like the powerful spirits of both his parents, have brought out the best in him and it shines through the pages of this loving portrait of the kind, generous, funny, brave, beautiful woman his mother was. John and June would have been proud.

— KRIS KRISTOFFERSON

Writin' such a beautiful book about his own mama is a great gift John Carter has given to her memory, and to the world. Sharing these memories with all of us is so special, and I love John Carter Cash for doing this.

— LORETTA LYNN

Anchored in Love is extraordinarily courageous and meticulously truthful, written in a graceful, poignant narrative that serves and illuminates my stepmother's life. Although he may not have intended it to be so, the book is ultimately a testament to my brother. He writes without self-pity and with a clarity and objectivity that is startling—and commendable. I thought I knew my family pretty well. I learned more in these pages.

— ROSANNE CASH

What a loving portrait you have written about your mother. I'm so proud of you . . . She's proud of you too. I'm grateful to God that I was a small part of her life . . . She was, and is, a big part of mine.

— LARRY GATLIN

June Carter lived literally her whole life on a stage. To her fans, she was the sassy, saucy singing partner and soul mate to one of music's greatest icons. To herself, she was the self-designated matriarch and keeper of country music's most revered family name. But behind the "Country Girl" persona was an enormously complex and often-tormented woman. Although she played for presidents and princes on the great music stages of the world, the reality of her life was not always so exalted. Only one person could possibly peel back the layers and take us into the shadows of this lady. In this extraordinary account, John Carter Cash chronicles a life of destiny and despair as seen through a son's eyes—and heart. Be prepared to smile and celebrate. And to cry. For while history will forever define June by her role as Johnny Cash's queen consort, you will learn that there were tears on that crown. This is a unique, compelling look into the high price June Carter Cash paid for her name.

— MARK STIELPER
Historian, writer, family friend

Anchored in Love

Anchored in Love

AN INTIMATE PORTRAIT
OF JUNE CARTER CASH

JOHN CARTER CASH

THOMAS NELSON
Since 1798

NASHVILLE   DALLAS   MEXICO CITY   RIO DE JANEIRO   BEIJING

ANCHORED IN LOVE

Published in Nashville, Tennessee, by Thomas Nelson, Inc.

Thomas Nelson, Inc. titles may be purchased in bulk for educational, business, fundraising, or sales
promotional use. For information, please e-mail SpecialMarkets@thomasnelson.com.

Scripture quotations used in this book are from The Holy Bible, New International Version (NIV).
Copyright © 1973, 1978, 1984, International Bible Society. Used by permission of Zondervan Bible
Publishers.

For more information go to johncartercash.com or junecartercash.com.

Editorial team: Kate Etue, Sue Ann Jones, Alice Sullivan, Lori Jones, Recah Theodosiou.

Cover design by Gina Binkley, altarego design.

Cover photo by © Alan Messer/www.alanmesser.com

Page design by Walter Petrie

Library of Congress Cataloging-in-Publication Data

Cash, John Carter.
    Anchored in love : an intimate portrait of June Carter Cash / John Carter Cash.
      p. cm.
    Includes bibliographical references
    ISBN-10 0-8499-0187-1 (HC)
    ISBN-13 978-0-8499-0187-4 (HC)
    ISBN-10 0-8499-1907-X (IE)
    ISBN-13 978-0-8499-1907-7 (IE)

    1. Cash, June Carter, 1929–2003. 2. Cash, Johnny. 3. Country musicians—United States—
Biography. I. Title.
ML420.C2653C67 2007
782.421642092—dc22
[B]   2007007636

Printed in the United States of America

07 08 09 10 11 QW 9 8 7 6 5 4 3 2 1

To my children,

Anna Maybelle, Joseph John, and Jack Ezra Cash.

And to my wife, Laura.

Press on . . .

Keep on the sunny side,
Always on the sunny side.
Keep on the sunny side of life.
It will help us ev'ry day,
It will brighten all the way,
If we keep on the sunny side of life.

— A. P. CARTER
"Keep on the Sunny Side"
Recorded by
the Original Carter Family
May 9–10, 1928

Contents

Foreword

BY ROBERT DUVALL

When I first met June Carter Cash, I was immediately embraced by her warmth, her charisma, and her generosity (something I'm convinced all "first timers" experienced). From those initial meetings, many wonderful friendships flourished and grew.

I have always felt, and still feel, that I was a friend of June's.

She was (and in memory still is) a true child of the beautiful mountain region of rural, southwest Virginia who became a devoted wife, a mother, and a national and international performer.

Deep religious convictions served June in all aspects of her life—and what an active life! And what a sense of humor! The family always came first: her husband John, son John Carter, and her other grown children.

I can well remember June cooking her famous "mater" (tomato) dumplings or helping John fix his tall, nightly glass of cold buttermilk with a big chunk of cornbread floating in it before he went off to bed. I remember well when June would amuse us all with the dancing of a jig or the mountain flat foot. Her humor was always in evidence—an entertainer at home and abroad.

I hope all of those who knew June feel as blessed as I do at having known her because we were all able to share a portion of her life.

The memory of this wonderful mountain woman will be remembered through the ages and will most certainly live and relive into the future in my memory.

Her grace is far-reaching.

Acknowledgments

When Kate Etue and David Moberg from Thomas Nelson Publishers suggested that I write about my mother's life, I was apprehensive and hesitant. How could I do my mother justice in fifty thousand words? How could I tell a comprehensive tale of a life so strong, diverse, and influential? As her son, how could I remove myself enough from her legacy to be truly objective? Most worrisome, how could I honestly tell her story without speaking of the dark times, of her shortcomings and addictions, without seeming angry or betraying some sadness I would rather keep hidden?

If I was going to write her biography, I wanted the story to focus on her positive legacy, on a life well lived. But at the same time I had to be honest. I hope I've done that in these pages; I hope I've shown how her light pierced the darkness of the difficult times. Most importantly, I hope I've shown how the greatest legacy she left behind was love and forgiveness, strong family bonds, and a deep appreciation for home.

I would prefer that when my children and grandchildren want to know who their grandmother was, that they find the personality and story of June Carter Cash in this book, written by someone within the family who loved her, rather than (with all due respect to historians and masters of biographical writing) in a work penned by an author who knew her only through scholarly research.

One of the greatest tasks I faced in putting Mom's story together was to write about her life before I was born. I felt I could offer only so much insight into who she was before I came along. My family's close friends Lou and Karen Robin were tremendously helpful to me in collecting this information. Lou managed my parents' careers for nearly thirty years while they were still alive, and he continues to protect and safeguard their legacy today.

At the same time, I must point out that, while I hope I've stayed true to the facts in writing about my mother's family and career, sometimes the sources I consulted conflicted with each other, making me wonder what dates, places, and sequences should be put with particular events. Sometimes the way I remembered something through personal experience was different from what Mom wrote about in her own books, *Among My Klediments* and *From the Heart,* or what others wrote in books about our family. So I ask the reader to keep in mind that this is *not* a scholarly work but more of a memoir, a personal, from-the-heart account of what I remember or have been told about my mother.

I am especially indebted to my sisters, most greatly to Carlene Carter and Rosanne Cash, whose memories and words are an important part of this book. Janette Carter, Joyce Trayweek, and Rosemary Edelman were likewise invaluable to me as I put the tale together. Without the insight and memories of all these beloved women, this book would never have been completed. I must also offer considerable thanks to Fern Salyer, who has in essence adopted me since my mother's passing. She is truly the closest living thing to my mother in heart and spirit. I love you, Fern. Thank you.

Thanks also to Mark Stielper, Bob Sullivan, Cathy Sullivan, and especially Lisa Kristofferson. I am grateful for your help.

And to Sue Ann Jones: thanks for sticking with me through this process. Thanks for helping to put some order to my writings and for all your suggestions, amendments, and corrections. This book would not be if not for your help, patience, and guidance.

Likewise, this book would never have happened if not for my wife, Laura. Her support through the deaths of my parents and sister was God's strength coming to me through her. She has also brought to my spirit a flourishing desire to better know my roots, and with it, a true appreciation for my family history. Thank you, my love. You have shown me my purpose for life.

There are many who were close to Mom and who influenced her life through the years—Colonel Tom Parker; the Frank Clement family; Michelle Rollins and her husband, the late John Rollins; Jane Seymour and James Keach; Jessi Colter; Willie and Annie Nelson, to name a few. There are also many who had an impact on her life who are not mentioned in these pages. I offer my apologies and ask that this book be accepted for what it really is: my mother, seen through my eyes.

Writing this book has been a beautiful experience for me, remembering these memories, good and bad. The grief of losing her physical presence from my life has been eased by this work because it has brought me close to her again, close to the best of her. She has taken on new life to me in these pages. I hope you also sense her spirit in this story.

John Carter Cash

PROLOGUE

Angel of Appalachia

So wear a happy smile and life will be worthwhile.
Forget the tears and don't forget to smile.
You are my flower that's blooming in the mountain,
You are my flower that's blooming there for me.

— A. P. CARTER
"You Are My Flower"
Recorded by
the Original Carter Family
June 8, 1938

The Holston River winds through the valleys of southwestern Virginia like a great slumbering snake. The month of June can be hot in this part of the world, and today is one of those days. The water is still cool, though, despite the sun beating down on our heads. Along the river banks, the crickets and frogs sing in chorus to accompany the steady rustle of water and wind.

Since I am the heaviest, I sit in the back of the massive flat-bottom boat; my cousin Shane Salyer is in the middle seat, and my wife, Laura, is in the front, resting uncomfortably on the metal bench. She is eight and a half months pregnant. My son Joseph sits beside her.

"Not again," I moan as the boat comes to a scraping halt atop the shallow limestone riverbed. The water isn't all that low, really, but it's slow moving. We had opted for the largest and most stable boat (a safety precaution for the pregnant lady) but had quickly found it was also the heaviest. Shane and I had already had to get out three times and drag the tub across the shallows. Laura is brave, smart, stubborn, and tough; however, she is evidently beginning to tire of this debacle.

"Out of the way, kids!" yells brother-in-law Jimmy Tittle as he glides past us in his one-man canoe. He turns quickly and splashes a burst of paddle water playfully in our direction. The water cools my face and shoulders.

"Hey now!" says Shane, also dampened by the assault. He splashes back ferociously.

I grab my paddle, and we mount an all-out splash attack. Jimmy responds with the desperate exuberance one would expect of a lone renegade. Laura covers her head with my discarded shirt and waits for the battle to die down. Before long, we are all soaked.

This week is a rare occurrence, with almost the entire Cash-Carter clan gathered in Maces Springs, Virginia. Earlier this year, every grandchild received the following letter:

The Patriarch
of the Cash and Carter Family Clans
cordially, joyously, and lovingly invites You,
the Grandchildren, the Honorees,
to a weeklong Clinch Mountain Celebration
June 17–24,
cumulating on Sunday, June 23, the 72nd birthday of
Lady June Carter Cash.

Herewith it is hereby and thereby proclaimed,

ascertained, and declared, that the life and talents,

attributes, and dispositions

of Lady Cash are

Unique and Extraordinary.

Lady Cash,

being wholly deserving of her title,

having descended by matrimonial decree from

Ada, Queen of Scots,

sister of King Malcolm IV.

(Ada's Queendom covered

all of what is now County Fife, Scotland.)

Trails and hiking,

up and down beautiful Clinch Mountain.

Food and sleeping,

if you so desire, for the whole week.

You, the Honorees,

are required, for the whole week,

to make necessary repairs

in the love lines of your Grandmother,

Lady June Carter Cash.

Musical wannabees, if you so desire,

pickin' on all four porches

of the late E. J. and Maybelle Carter home.

Saturday, the 23rd,

sleep late.

Afternoon birthday celebration for

Lady June Carter Cash, her 72nd.

After the birthday celebration,

the Honorees

are invited to attend

the Old Tyme Appalachian Project

known as the Carter Family Fold,

a musical program.

This program is morally good.

It is hosted by Joe and Janette Carter,

daughter and son of the original A.P. and Sara Carter.

Come one! Come all!

Sixteen Grandchildren all,

And one Great-Grandchild.

Come, children, come.

Bring a parent to help you if you need.

But this week is yours,

Grandchildren

of the Lady June Carter Cash.

John R Cash

Patriarch

of the Cash and Carter Family Clans

Most of the grandkids obliged and brought their parents to pay homage.

All my life I have come here with *my* parents. Although they own a number of houses, this valley—known as Clinch Valley, Poor Valley, or "Pore" Valley, as Mom always calls it—is home to them in a way nowhere else is. This is where my mother was born, and where she still finds comfort. Here, she is a child again.

The old family home sits at the base of the vast Clinch Mountain, a huge limestone outcropping that runs from Middle Tennessee up into Virginia. My grandparents, Ezra and Maybelle Addington Carter, lived in the house in the 1930s. Although it slipped out of the immediate family briefly after their deaths, my parents managed to buy it back in the 1970s.

Today we are partaking in the long-celebrated tradition of floating the Holston River, which runs not far from the house. My sister Rosanne, her husband John Leventhal, and their son Jake are in one canoe, basking in the sun and rowing gently. My sister Tara is in a canoe with her sons, Aran and Alex. Fred Schoebel, Tara's husband, and my brother-in-law Jimmy Tittle, Kathy's husband, are in one-man canoes.

The day is wearing on, and thoughts of the cool homeplace are beginning to beckon.

As we round a bend in the river, my sister Rosanne bursts out laughing. I follow her gaze to a figure in the distance wearing a long white dress and large sun hat, and waving some kind of little flag. This angelic image will be recalled to my mind many times in the years to come.

"Oh, children, be careful! Is everyone wearing their life jackets?" my mother calls out from the riverbank. Although care is evident in her voice, joy is even more apparent. "Oh, I wish I could be on those rafts with you!" she calls yearningly.

There is light and laughter in her voice, a deep and resounding tone of youth and nostalgia. This river is as much a part of her as are the mountains and the music of her family. Having all of us here is, to her, the unbroken circle of a long-lasting legacy. We are all her babies, as she lovingly calls us. Her heart and love have brought us together here. Her heart is as big and steadfast as Clinch Mountain, and her love for us is as strong as an April thunderstorm, as tender as the westerly breeze slipping gently through the valley.

We drift past her, waving and laughing.

PART 1

A Daughter of the Mountains

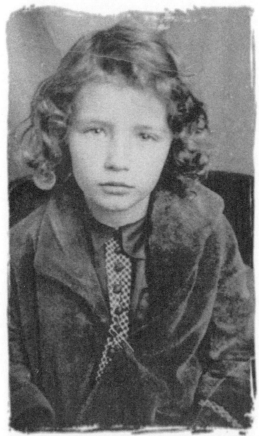

June Carter, age five.

ONE

The Music of the Mountains

Just a village and a homestead on the farm,
A mother's love to shield you from all harm,
A mother's love so true, and a sweetheart brave and true,
A village and a homestead on the farm.

— A. P. CARTER
"Homestead on the Farm"
Recorded by
the Original Carter Family
November 22–24, 1929

Mom and I were sitting on the porch of the Virginia house. She was talking, and mostly I was just listening, an arrangement that was quite common in our relationship. She always had a lot to say. I was in my late teens and was eager to leave and go squirrel hunting with my cousin Shane. But Mom held me there a little while longer. She had another story to tell me.

"Your Grandfather Ezra was the first to bring electric power to this valley," she began . . .

Ezra Carter, also known as Eck, or Pop, was a descendant of some of the earliest and most fiercely independent settlers in Poor Valley, a little community at the foot of Clinch Mountain. He had grown up with four brothers and three sisters (another child died young) in a one-room cabin some two miles away from where Mom and I sat on the porch that day. In 1926 he married Maybelle Addington, a petite, sixteen-year-old beauty he'd met a few months earlier when she came from her home on the other side of the mountain to visit her first cousin, Sara Dougherty Carter. Like Ezra, Maybelle was descended from a long line of intrepid mountain folk, including a Revolutionary War veteran who settled in Virginia in 1773. Mom always liked to remind me that one of Grandma Maybelle's ancestors, Henry Addington, had been the prime minister of England.

For a while the newlyweds lived with Ezra's parents, Robert and Mollie Bays Carter, and their younger children in the Carters' tiny cabin. A short while later, Ezra built a slightly larger home nearby for him and Maybelle to move into. But their privacy didn't last long before his parents moved out of their old, weathered cabin and into the new house with Ezra and Maybelle. Although Ezra and Maybelle undoubtedly needed their privacy, love and unity of family were most important. I don't remember ever hearing about anyone disliking the arrangement.

Mom had often described my great-grandmother, Mollie Bays Carter, as a strong and vivacious character, a tough mountain lady with leathered hands and burdened back. She was an enthusiastic singer of songs; Mom used to say on Sundays you could hear Grandma Mollie singing a half mile away from the church, drowning out all the other voices. Mollie loved to dance; she could "cut a rug" dancing a jig. And she had an intense faith in God.

She was also a midwife who attended the home births of many of her own grandchildren, including Helen, Maybelle and Ezra's first child, born September 19, 1927.

It was the custom in those days for people to share music both at home with their families and in community "conventions," "schools," and performances. Sometimes while they visited on each other's porches someone would pull out a fiddle or a banjo and sing for friends and neighbors. Other times music lovers scheduled singing meetings or held special events in schoolhouses and other community centers. Sometimes a hat might be passed to collect donations for the performers' benefit; other times a token fee was charged at the door. Music was a strong, beautiful thread that tied the people of the mountains to their traditions, history, and folklore. Not everyone in the mountains had a gift for making music, but almost everyone had a love for hearing it.

Eleven years before Ezra and Maybelle were married, Maybelle's cousin Sara Dougherty had married Ezra's older brother, Alvin Pleasant Carter (known as A.P. or Doc). Sara had a beautiful voice and could play the autoharp, the guitar, and the banjo. A.P. was a jittery man who could never sit still. Mollie Carter had been pregnant with A.P. and was standing under a tree when it was struck by lightning; she always blamed her son's constant, lifelong fidgeting and shaking on that prenatal incident.

During their brief marriage, Sara and A.P. had discovered that folks were willing to pay a little money to hear Sara sing. And when she occasionally performed with her cousin Maybelle, who had a unique style of guitar playing, picking out the melody and strumming the rhythm simultaneously, the resulting music was something people remembered and talked about. Occasionally, A.P. jumped in to join them with his inimitable bass vocals.

In the summer of 1927, A.P. noticed an ad in the Bristol, Tennessee, newspaper announcing that the Victor Company was bringing a recording machine to town for a few days. A.P. was excited to learn that the record company's agent would pay an amazing fifty dollars for every song deemed worthy of recording.

By then Sara was the mother of three—eight-year-old Gladys, five-year-old Janette, and infant Joe—and Maybelle was eight and a half months pregnant with Helen. In an interview before she died in 2006, Janette told me about that day in 1927 when the carload of Carters set off without her to audition for the recording company in Bristol.

"The car was full," she said. "It was Mommy and Maybelle and Daddy and Gladys—she went to tend to Joe. I still remember standin' at that gate, a-screamin' and a-cryin' why they couldn't take me.

"Daddy said to Mommy, 'What *is* wrong with that young'n? She's a-screamin' and a-cryin'. Why are you leavin' her here? Take her. You're takin' the rest.'

"And Mommy said, 'No, there just ain't room for us all.' And they left me. I've never forgot them a-runnin' off and leavin' me and takin' the others," Janette said.

It took A.P. all day to drive Ezra's borrowed, jam-packed car over the sweltering, twenty-five miles of unpaved roads from the Carters' homes at Maces Springs, near Hiltons, to Bristol. There, in a makeshift studio, the three of them performed for Victor agent Ralph Peer, who ended up recording six of their songs and paying them three hundred dollars.

They went back home to Maces Springs and heard nary a word about their recordings—until several months later when Ezra and Maybelle happened to be in town and heard what turned out to be the Carter Family's first phonograph record being played over a store's loudspeaker.

The outside world was beginning to hear the music that had wafted through the Appalachian Mountains for generations, the same ballads and hymns and whimsical verses that had filled the Carters' homes daily.

In addition to remarkable musical talent, there also was great humor and laughter in the Carter clan. According to Janette, her mother, Sara, was quite a prankster. Sara's most famous escapade occurred one day when Maybelle had put her new baby to sleep and had gone outside to get water from the well just a few yards from the door. While Maybelle was away, Sara sneaked in and took the baby, cradle and all, and hid the quiet, slumbering child high in the closet. Maybelle returned, found the child missing, and according to Janette, "fainted dead away."

She was hurriedly revived to the sound of Sara's mischievous laughter. With rascally delight, Sara lowered the cradle into Maybelle's arms as the distraught young mother, still a teenager at that point, furiously and tearfully admonished Sara. It may have been upsetting at the time, but this kind of family humor and teasing were common among the Carters. A love of laughter and comedy would later become most obvious in the spirit of Eck and Maybelle's fun-loving middle child, June.

The first songs recorded by A.P., Sara, and my Grandma Maybelle were well received, and soon the three began recording more music under contract with Victor. Maybelle was recognized as the most talented guitar player in the family, while Sara had the strongest voice and played the autoharp as they sang. In the fall of 1928, Maybelle became pregnant once again, and the baby within her must have heard the steady rhythm of the guitar daily, must have been attuned to the sound of Appalachian music coursing through her bones and muscle from her earliest moments. With her Grandma Mollie serving as midwife, Valerie June Carter was born on June 23, 1929, in Maces Springs, Virginia, into what would become known as the First Family of Country Music.

Grandma Maybelle was a devoted mother, but she had trouble producing enough breast milk for baby June, perhaps because by that time she had to travel frequently to perform and record with A.P. and Sara. As a result, June spent quite a bit of time at the bosom of her Aunt Ora, the wife of Eck's brother Ermine Carter. At the other breast was June's first cousin Fern. This was common practice in those days, since there were no supermarkets or baby formula.

Recently Fern recalled a memory her mother often shared about how that came to happen: "When June and I were both little babies, Mama said to Aunt Maybelle one day, 'That child don't look like she's gettin' enough milk.' And Aunt Maybelle said, 'I don't think she is.' Mama said, 'Well, just let me nurse *her* too.' See, Mama was nursing me, and she had so much milk she couldn't handle it all. So she nursed June and me both, and she kept June a lot when Maybelle was working." The close bond that began between June and Fern as infants would last a lifetime.

By 1929, the Carter Family—A.P., Sara, and Maybelle—were becoming increasingly popular and traveling around the country performing their music. When they came home from their travels, A.P. would leave again for weeks at a time, usually traveling alone, searching the hills for folks to visit and songs to record.

By 1933, when their third daughter, Anita, was born, Ezra and Maybelle had moved into a large home just over the hill from Mollie and Robert. It was on the porch of this house where Mom and I were sitting that day. Mom's Virginia childhood home was a place we visited as often as we could.

To us, it has always felt like sacred ground.

Mom described Grandpa Eck as a resourceful, deep-thinking man who loved tinkering and working with his hands. He always saw intriguing possibilities where others saw difficulties. He supported and believed in Maybelle's music and her amazing ability to play her guitar, but he had his own career, and as Mom liked to point out, he was an important man in the valley. He worked as a railroad postal agent, collecting, sorting, and delivering the mail along the train route from Bristol to Washington, DC.

His job either required or allowed him (I'm not sure which) to carry a gun. He was exceedingly intelligent, able to memorize hundreds of postal codes, addresses, and routes, and he was also inventive when it came to ways to spread his paycheck around the valley. He hired others to work for him at assorted projects and jobs, some of which may have seemed a bit outlandish at the time. His three daughters grew up watching him help his neighbors and share his blessings, and they learned to do the same.

Eck loved to read, and apparently he was inspired by what he read about the latest developments with electricity. He even dammed up the little creek that ran alongside their house and somehow put together a contraption that could generate electricity to light up their nine-room residence. That's how the Carter home became the first to have electricity in Poor Valley. But it wasn't enough. Eck wanted more.

Just more than a mile from Maybelle and Ezra's home, as the crow flies, the Holston River runs, strong and constant. Between the house and river, however, there are two quite tall, mountainous ridges, or "knobs," as they're known in that area. Others might have seen the rugged landscape as an impediment between them and the river. Grandpa Ezra, a man of vision, saw possibility.

Unbelievably, he built a dam across the Holston River and constructed a large turbine to generate electricity. Then he ran a line from the turbine over the knobs to his home (and apparently to a couple of neighbors' homes too). Before long, the power company in Bristol bought him out, and soon electricity was available to a wider area. But it was Grandpa Eck who first brought it to the valley. That's the story Mom told me that afternoon as we sat on the porch.

I really can't remember how our time together ended that day. Maybe I was impatient to get into the woods, standing and pacing as Mom neared the end of the story. Maybe I stayed longer, enjoying getting to spend some quiet time with her. Either way, as I think back on that long-ago afternoon, I can feel the peace of that quiet homeplace embracing me once more. Things were different there. They still are. And we are different when we are there.

June Carter left the Poor Valley at a young age to travel the world. Yet somehow it stayed within her throughout her life, whether she was performing before thousands on the other side of the globe or talking with the girl at the grocery-store checkout . . . whether she was dining with the president and first lady in the White House or having dinner with her cousin Joe Carter back in Maces Springs . . . whether she was flying in a little Cessna 180 over the Alaskan wilderness or entertaining the troops in a war zone or meeting the U.S. ambassador in Poland . . . wherever she was, whatever she was doing, she was, at heart, the same endearing, simple mountain girl she'd always been. Her first cousin Ester Moore said June was "always happy, always full of herself. It seemed like everyone wanted to be around her."

She was kind and generous, humorous and excitable, loyal and strong. One of her friends, Lisa Kristofferson, would say about her later, "June was a bright, sparkling star . . . universal love made incarnate in a pretty, talented, frisky package."

This girl from Poor Valley would change in many ways after she left the mountains and went on to what some would describe as great success. But her heart, her character, remained unchanged. Throughout her life she would try and succeed, try and fail, try again. She would enjoy success while enduring great heartache and greater loss. And through it all, she never lost her identity as a simple, God-fearing child of the mountains. She knew no other way.

TWO

The World Beyond

Some people sing for money—
not me, I do it for spite . . .

The style this year is one-piece bathing suits.
I've got a new two-piece—
and I can't figure out which piece to wear.

Handwritten notes for
June's comedy sketches,
recorded in her "ledger"

Music came naturally to at least two of Eck and Maybelle's daughters. Early in life, Helen picked up the guitar and learned from her mother how to play it. At the age of three, Anita showed great promise as a singer and musician. June, the middle child, was something else.

Energetic and good humored, she worked hard and played even harder. According to her cousin Fern, June was a tomboy, always bringing home lost animals and playing in the creek, happiest when she was in mud up to her waist.

In her 1979 book, *Among My Klediments,* Mom described her childhood this way:

I grew up being afraid to wear make-up, afraid to dance, afraid to wear a basketball suit because it wasn't modest. . . .

Then, life to me was four square miles of going to grandmother's, over to aunts' and uncles', worming tobacco, hoeing corn, and milking cows. It was a world of pawpaws, chinka-pins, and huckleberries. Somewhere out there, over the mountains, there was a world I'd only seen in books. It was full of hamburgers, ice cream cones, and movie stars. Out there the preacher let you play basketball, and you could buy a real tube of lipstick—and you could dance. Somewhere over that mountain I could dance and it would be all right.[1]

June did not exhibit the same natural musical abilities as her two sisters. She was clearly the most outspoken and outgoing of the three, so she definitely had the personality for performing, but by the time she was five years old, she could barely carry a tune. She learned to sing anyway, compensating for her lack of musical ability by making audiences laugh with her down-home enthusiasm and cornpone jokes. She put her heart into any performance and drew laughs with her quick wit.

By the time June was nine years old, her mother had been singing and recording with the Original Carter Family eleven years. While the Carters' music was enjoyed by thousands of people outside the family, to June it was as common as the sun rising over the hollow, as much a part of her life as her own mother's voice. In the winter of 1938–1939, however, the Carter Family would step into an even larger realm of popularity when A.P., Sara, and Maybelle moved to Del Rio, Texas, for six months to perform twice-daily music shows on the famous radio station XERA.

According to Mark Zwonitzer's book *Will You Miss Me When I'm Gone?* XERA broadcast through an astounding five-hundred-thousand-watt transmitter located just south of the Mexican border (to avoid the American government's two-hundred-thousand-watt limit). There were no international broadcasting laws then, and it was said that XERA's signal could be heard throughout North America, as far away as Chicago; Washington, DC; and even Montreal. Mom used to joke that you could hear that radio station in your dental fillings and mattress springs. She insisted that many folks reported hearing the station simply by standing next to a barbed-wire fence and listening carefully, even on a windy day.

XERA was owned by Dr. John Romulus Brinkley, an entrepreneur from Kansas who had made a fortune through the practice of surgically implanting goat glands in older men who were desperate to improve their stamina and sexual performance. Brinkley sold many questionable articles through his broadcast station, including "signed" photos of Jesus and "pieces of the true cross." The government had refused to renew his broadcasting license after his operation was shut down in Kansas, so Brinkley had moved his production to the Texas-Mexico border, carefully placing his transmitters south of the Rio Grande.

The Carter Family and their music somehow transcended the quackery products and unethical procedures advertised by the radio station's owner. While Brinkley's raunchy claims raised eyebrows, the Carters, with their pure, mountain-born sound, were warmly welcomed as invited guests into homes with radios throughout America.

Amazingly, while their musical fame seemed to grow exponentially with every performance they sent out over the air waves, their private lives remained, for the most part, hidden. With the Carter Family's continent-wide radio program making them a household name, their popularity soared. Yet most listeners had no idea, as they listened to the Carters' melodic ballads and rugged tunes pouring out of the radio, what unspoken personal struggles were occurring. They had no idea that these glory years for the Original Carter Family would also be some of the last.

The fact was, although Sara and A.P. were still singing together with Maybelle, their marriage had ended.

A.P. had strived mightily to keep the musical group together, productive, and popular, but in doing so he had neglected his relationship with his wife. For years, he had been a rambler, leaving home for extended periods to look for new songs for Sara, Maybelle, and him to record and perform. Although A.P. was undeniably an accomplished composer in his own right, he was even more adept at recognizing and collecting marketable songs. He would sit on the porches of coal miners and black families, mountain people and hardscrabble farmers, copying lyrics and jotting down ideas for songs. The work was his passion. Unfortunately, it was not suited to maintaining a comfortable and supportive home life.

No one doubted that A.P. loved Sara. Yet, frequently left alone to keep the household running (especially difficult in those days of few modern conveniences), Sara had become increasingly sad and restless. Perhaps from exhaustion, or maybe because of what she saw happening to her family, she gradually lost interest in the traveling and the music. Coincidentally, she had also taken a "shine," as her daughter Janette put it, to Coy Bays, A.P.'s cousin, who, ironically, A.P. himself had asked to help out around the place while he was out collecting songs.

Coy and Sara spent a lot of time together, and their families apparently breathed a sigh of relief when Coy left the mountains in 1933 to help some of his family members who hoped to find relief for their tuberculosis out West. Despite his absence, though, Sara still pined for Coy.

A.P. wanted to keep the family together, both in front of the microphone and at home, but he eventually failed at both. The same year Coy left Virginia, Sara left her husband and children. She moved from the south side of Clinch Mountain back to the north side to live with Mil and Susie Nickels, the aunt and uncle who had raised Sara from childhood after her mother, Elizabeth Dougherty, died of typhoid. Sara and A.P.'s daughter Gladys tended to her younger siblings, Janette and Joe, and kept house for their daddy.

The couple officially divorced three years later, in 1936, but, amazingly, they continued to record with Maybelle as the Carter Family. And the group's popularity just kept on growing . . .

While the three Carters broadcast their music from Texas during the winter of 1938–1939, back in Virginia, their children and other relatives strained to hear their loved ones' familiar voices. Occasionally June even heard the voice of her little sister, Anita, deemed too young to be left behind. Maybelle had taken her youngest daughter to Texas with her while her older daughters, June and Helen, stayed behind with Eck and Grandma Carter.

Coy Bays, A.P.'s cousin and Sara's old flame, was listening to the Carters, too, from his new home in California. He and Sara apparently hadn't seen each other since Coy had left Virginia six years earlier, but they hadn't forgotten each other, either. One night in February 1939 while he was listening to the Carter Family's radio program, out of the blue, he heard Sara dedicate a song to him.

Coy promptly drove to Texas and married her.

Justifiably stunned by this unexpected turn of events, A.P. was released from the Carter Family's radio-music commitment a month early, and he headed back to Virginia, according to Zwonitzer. Sara and Maybelle finished out the radio contract, then Maybelle went home to the mountains to resume life with her husband and daughters, and Sara moved to California to live happily ever after with her new husband.

But before long the three were back in Texas with a new radio contract, and this time *all* the kids and husbands (and the ex-husband) came along. The latest technology allowed the Carters to record their music programs on "transcription disks" that could be delivered to the border-area radio stations for broadcasting. This meant the musicians could live in San Antonio rather than the more remote Del Rio.

It was there, in "San Antone," as Mom called it, that she ate her first ice cream cone. The year was 1939, she was ten years old, and apparently she and her sisters and cousins felt like they'd just moved to Mars. Mom loved to tell the story of how she bought some candy at the neighborhood store and stopped the store clerk cold when she asked him for a "poke." In *Among My Klediments,* she wrote, "No one could understand my Appalachian dialect, and I sure couldn't understand theirs. Finally I walked around the counter and picked up my poke and found out those silly people called it a paper bag."[2]

June missed the hills of Virginia, but she always carried tender memories of her time in Texas and Mexico throughout her life. She attended San Antonio's Hawthorne Junior High School, where she gave her first solo performance, singing "Old Engine 143" before the whole school while accompanying herself on the autoharp. She got her finger pick hung on the autoharp's string, and when she pulled, it flew across the stage.

Mom said she "never missed a word of the song," just kept on singing as she trotted across the stage, picked up the pick, and finished her song. "Engine 143 wrecked successfully and so did my stage debut," she wrote.[3] Reading her account of that "train wreck," you get the feeling a little light bulb went on in her head as the audience chuckled at her antics. Maybe she wasn't the family's most talented musician, but she could be funny, and an audience's hearty laughter was as welcome to Mom's ears as applause. She had learned a valuable lesson, and she eagerly shared it with me many years later. She told me we should always pray for God to help us be aware of our greatest gifts and to use them to the best of our ability throughout our lives. Mom learned to use beautifully and appealingly the gifts God had given her.

In San Antonio, Mom and her sisters and their cousin Janette also recorded for the radio program, as their parents did. She said they made transcriptions three days a week, and according to Zwonitzer, Maybelle's daughters were paid fifteen dollars each per week while Sara and A.P.'s Janette (who also had to help entertain and baby-sit her younger brother, Joe), got twenty. Although the Original Carter Family members—A.P.,

Sara, and Maybelle—were still the stars of the show, the next generation—
Helen, June, Anita, and Janette—helped fill out the musical programs.

By that time my Grandpa Eck had taken early retirement from his railroad postal job because of blood-pressure problems, and he had accompanied his family to Texas. While Eck never showed much musical ability
himself, he loved music, especially classical music, and he understood the
business potential of his wife and daughters' musical talent. While some
might have wrung their hands and worried about the musical future of the
Carter Family as they watched A.P. and Sara's marriage fall apart, Eck was,
no doubt, seeing possibility where others saw problems.

Mom wrote that while she and her sisters were in San Antonio recording for the Mexican-border radio stations, her mother "would never play
with us, only with Aunt Sara and Uncle Doc, so even if our performance
was bad we stood on our own and served our apprenticeship in the shadow
of the famous Carter Family."[4] Knowing how Grandpa Eck's clever mind
worked, I imagine he was watching his daughters' early performances,
encouraging and helping Maybelle groom them for the spotlight, and
thinking of ways they could build on the Carter Family's success if—or
rather, when—the Original Carter Family disbanded.

After their Texas radio work was done, the Carters loaded up their big
Packard and moved back to Virginia. Mom must have been about twelve
when they returned to the valley. She wrote that the return to Virginia
gave her a few years of life as "an ordinary girl"—if you can call it "ordinary" that her time was divided between church and school, farm chores,
playing on the basketball team (although she still worried that the short
uniform was so immodest she would go to hell for wearing it), working
the wheat with a thrashing machine, driving an overloaded log truck up
and down the hairpin curves of rough mountain roads, and singing with
her mother and sisters at churches, schools, courthouses, and auditoriums
all over the region.

Mom also wrote that during the summer when she turned fourteen, she begin riding "with Uncle Flan Bays and his children and friends . . . anywhere they had to sing because Uncle Flan taught singing school. . . . We'd go packed in the back of that old pickup, singing on the way to somewhere." Uncle Flan taught shaped-note music, and during that summer with her uncle and cousins, Mom wrote, "I finally learned to belt out a good clear alto."

She also had a born-again experience that summer. "I believe I've been one of the fortunate few who've seen the tongues of fire as on the day of Pentecost," she wrote. "The Holy Spirit did truly enter my body, change me, and make me a new person."[5]

Mom's faith didn't begin that day; she had been reared by a God-fearing mother and father who demonstrated a strong personal relationship with Jesus. Mom's born-again experience simply relaunched and renewed the faith she'd always had. It also delighted her mother, who, according to Mom, ran shouting through the house when she heard what had happened to June, "My heart is so happy!"

Mom's faith was always the most important element of her life, the foundation for everything else. Her cousin Ester Moore said Mom "had the strongest relationship with God of anyone I have ever known. . . . I have seen her troubled, I have seen her cry, but I always saw her get on her knees and pray." Mom's prayers for my dad, my sisters, and me were a constant component of our family's life. In her journal she wrote some of her "daily prayers," as she called them. One of them said simply:

Thank you, oh, Lord, for all the wonderful things of this day. Thank you for all my blessings. Use me in any way you see fit. Amen.

About this time, Ezra took over the professional management and booking for his family, who became known as Mother Maybelle and the Carter

Sisters. At Eck's insistence, Anita, the baby, took to playing the upright bass (standing on something—a chair, a box, or a suitcase—to do it), and Helen, the oldest and already an accomplished guitarist, took up the accordion.

Zwonitzer tells the funny story of how Helen complained about having to learn the accordion, because she said it made no sense: "This thing is just absolutely backwards to the piano." She hated having to play the melody with her left hand and the lower octaves with her right. Somehow, though, she managed to do it—until they played a date in Louisville, where Pee Wee King told Helen, "Did you know you've got that on upside down?"[6]

Mom was the one with all the charm and energy, fire and spirit. She played the autoharp, and she danced and sang and laughed. Audiences loved Mother Maybelle and her daughters, but they especially loved the feisty little pigtailed "Juney" Carter with her corny jokes, ridiculous character portrayals, and savvy skills for promoting the sponsor's products. She was beginning a lifetime of performing and entertaining.

I don't know what Mom hoped for her future at that stage of her life. Whatever her dreams were, though, they could not have been big enough, or grand enough, to predict the life this mountain girl would someday live.

THREE

Not Like the Other Girls

Richmond girl, Richmond girl,
You've got your golden tresses
Twisted neatly into curls.
The pride of the south is in you,
You queen of the Old Dominion.
You're a proper southern lady,
Richmond girl.

—JOHNNY CASH
"Richmond Girl"

Mom always joked with mock dismay that World War II knocked the Carter Family off the cover of *Life* magazine. The big-city photographer had come to Maces Springs and snapped pictures for the photo feature, and twelve-year-old June was excited about the prospect of appearing on the cover of one of the most widely read magazines in the world at that time. But it never happened. The problem, Mom would explain, was that, wouldn't you know, the Japanese chose *their* week, the Carters' week—the week of December 7, 1941—to bomb Pearl Harbor. I don't think Mom ever forgave them. (Many years later, long after all three members of the Original Carter Family were laid to rest, *Life* did finally print the photos and article, but the ones who started it all never knew.)

Mom and her family didn't stay home in the valley for long. In the fall of 1942, the Original Carter Family signed a contract with fifty-thou-sand-watt WBT Radio in Charlotte, North Carolina, the city that would become June's next home away from home. According to Zwonitzer, Sara rode the train from California to sing with A.P. and Maybelle, and once again Maybelle's daughters and other family members filled out the daily programs headlined by the Original Carter Family.

Courtesy of John Layton Harlin

A poster advertising the Carter Sisters' performance highlights June's effervescent personality.

There was a housing shortage in Charlotte due to the war, so the family lived in the Roosevelt Hotel. It was in Charlotte that Mom went out on her first date. "That young man just marched right into the Roosevelt Hotel, straight up to my daddy, and asked him," Mom wrote in *Among My Klediments*. "I'd never been so scared in my life. No one asked my father anything, except maybe whether he had gotten his *Bristol Herald* or not. Most young men were frightened to death of him."[1]

The young man was so confident, Mom said, Grandpa Eck gave in—and also agreed to another young man who asked Helen out. They had a double date "to a ball game—in a car of all things," Mom wrote.[2] I do not know who Mom's date was, but certainly Helen's was Glenn Jones, her future husband and only true boyfriend.

The Original Carter Family continued to make music together until the Charlotte contract expired in March 1943. Then, says Zwonitzer, "the Original Carter Family disbanded for good."[3]

Mom wrote that she left Charlotte "kicking and screaming and clinging to friends I'd never forget."[4] But she enjoyed living in Richmond, Virginia, their next home, even more. The next generation was ready to take center stage.

Not that Mother Maybelle and the Carter Sisters immediately moved into an equally bright spotlight as the Original Carter Family had occupied. Their three-year "gig" in Richmond, Virginia, started out on the tiny, five-thousand-watt WRNL station; later they would move up to Richmond's larger WRVA. They also performed on the radio station's Saturday night show, *Old Dominion Barn Dance*, broadcast from the Lyric Theater. Maybelle and her girls supplemented their radio work with some live performances that Eck arranged for them throughout the area.

In 2002, when Mom and I began to work on her *Wildwood Flower* CD, she gave me a copy of several of their WRNL performances. Mom's voice is easy to distinguish from the other girls' as she sings resolutely and enthusiastically—and totally out of pitch.

Mom credited Richmond with giving the family "five good years. . . . God was good to us, and Mother, Helen, Anita, Daddy, and I were bound with a love you can't write on paper."[5]

In Richmond, Mom enrolled in John Marshall High School and "began to learn to be a Richmond girl," she wrote. "I said good-bye to the girl in coveralls and billed cap. My days of logging were over. It was a time of growing up to be a cultured southern lady. . . . What a wonderful year!"[6]

Becoming a Richmond girl meant learning how to ride, so Maybelle enrolled Helen and Mom at the Richmond Riding Academy. Assuring the instructor she knew how to ride (but failing to mention that her previous mounts had been the "old plugs from the farms in the valley"), Mom climbed onto the back of a mare and noticed, just before the horse set off at a run, that "the saddle had no horn."

It was her first experience with English-style riding, and as she would do in so many other situations where her skill might not have measured up to others' expectations, she turned calamity into comedy.

Here's how she described one of those early riding sessions:

I had just learned that if I stood up, then sat down, at least I'd stay on top of the horse instead of around the side where I'd been hanging for the last fifteen minutes.

Then I heard the horn. I couldn't believe it. Across the road darted the dogs, the hunters after them, all following a fox, and my horse decided to get into the chase. Canter—canter. Since I'd only learned a minute ago how to keep from falling off, I decided the best thing for me to do was to hold on to the mane. Pray, post, and scream. I did all those very well. And all I could see was my very excited horse fast after the pack, with blue sky and sunshine between me and the saddle.[7]

Such a wild beginning might have terrified a less daring soul, but for Mom, it was "the beginning of my love for riding."

She made more lifelong friends in Richmond, including her favorite high school pal, Joyce Blair Dobbins (now Joyce Trayweek). Joyce remembers the first time she saw June Carter at John Marshall High School: "She had freckles dancing off her face. She was scrubbed and shiny like a new penny." While Mom enjoyed her work on stage and on the radio, as a fifteen-year-old high school senior, she couldn't help but wish her life could be more like Joyce's.

"I just wanted to be like all the other girls in that school," Mom wrote in her book *From the Heart*. "I wanted to go to dances, have dates, see the ball games, go to pep rallies, hang out after church with the crowd, meet at Hotchkiss Field to watch football practice, have an ice cream soda at the drugstore, and ride home on the streetcar with my best friend. I wanted to do all those things Joyce did and all the other lucky girls."

And, she wrote, "I wanted to be a sponsor—there were only ten—for our Cadet Corps."[8] Joyce was already a sponsor—and the girlfriend of one of the captains of the Cadet Corps.

One thing Joyce and Mom had in common was their Christian beliefs, and both of them clung fervently to the power of prayer throughout their lives. Back then they prayed that Mom would get to be a sponsor for the Cadet Corps too. As a result, Mom wrote, "the only good-looking, unattached captain in that Cadet Corps walked up to me and, without knowing why, Captain Bobby Spires asked me to be his sponsor."

Mom called it "the miracle of prayer, that good God heard such a silly little girl and her insignificant prayer. I never forgot it."[9]

June graduated from John Marshall in 1946, and she cried because she wasn't going on to college like Joyce and her other friends. Joyce said later, "June had such a dream for going on with academics. A good portion of her homework was done in the backseat of Maybelle's car or backstage. Her father wanted her to go on with the traveling show . . . Ezra knew that if she went on to college, the family never would have a career without her."

Mom may have thought she could do it all, go to college and continue with the family's music, but apparently her dad convinced her otherwise. "I couldn't understand why it was more important for me to work," she wrote. "But it was. Our family was a unit. . . . So we had our homemade college— the guitar, the songs, the road work, putting up public address systems, and the discipline of our parents." Her homegrown graduate education taught her to "sing all the parts, take up tickets at the door, drive all over the USA, and do what was necessary to make a good show," she wrote.[10]

Mom always taught me that "the show must go on." She lived this way her whole life, and it was surely during this period that her devout work ethic was formed. Later in her life, it would be the motivation behind one of the best-known eruptions in her early work with Dad before they were married.

She had performed in Albuquerque with Johnny Cash and his road show, and after the show, he had disappeared. This was normal behavior for him then, since he was always looking to get into something, or pursue his insatiable wanderlust. As Mom said in a 1980 interview with Johnny Carson, "Johnny Cash was being *Cash*."

When it was time to leave for the airport that morning, the boys in the band told Mom they couldn't get Dad to wake up and get out of bed. They all worried they were going to miss their flight to El Paso for that night's show. In the *Tonight Show* interview, Mom described the incident, telling Carson, "I thought, *My momma wouldn't like this a bit. . . . We've got to play tonight.*"

Mom knew she had to confront Dad. "I thought, *Well, he can fire me, but I really don't care. We've got to play El Paso*, because that's what Mother would have said."

Somehow band member Marshall Grant managed to get Dad's room key, and Mom found him "lying there with the covers over his head," she told Carson. "I said, 'John, well, you know, we're going to miss the plane. C'mon.'"

Dad answered, "I'm not going; I feel awful. I just feel awful," and pulled the covers back up over his head.

Mom said, "I stood there, and I prayed a bit and wondered what else I should do." Finally she opened the door to his room and "hollered, just as hard as I could holler, 'Okay, lay there, star!' And that's all it took."

Mom said Dad "came out of bed" wearing nothing but his undershorts— "and we hadn't gotten that far along yet!" She ran for dear life to the car, where the others were waiting. "The only way he could get to me was to get his britches on and get out to the car," she told Carson. "We took off for the airport and I thought, *Well, it's the last of my Johnny Cash days. . . . I'm gonna be fired, but it's all right. I did what I had to do.*"

At the airport, as Mom waited in the coffee shop for their plane, Dad came in looking really mad. Mom thought, *This is gonna be it*. Then she noticed (remember, they were in Albuquerque), Dad was smoking a peace pipe. He had bought it in the airport gift shop. He handed it to her and said, "Peace."

It was apparently a turning point in their relationship. They made the show that night in El Paso. Knowing the condition Dad was in, it probably wasn't pretty. But the show *did* go on, thanks to the strong sense of responsibility Mom had learned from her own show-performing mother.

That summer after her high school graduation, Mom and her family went home to Virginia and worked the "old circuits [that] sometimes called for five shows a day," she said. "I learned to sleep in the car, get ready in five minutes, and tune a guitar in two." It was an exhausting lifestyle, but then, Mom wrote, "I stopped a show with a routine, and I finally had to face it—I was hooked."[11] The fact was, there could be no other life for her, no denying her heritage. Within her, she held the soul of an entertainer and the blood of a musician, and her future was calling.

Following a brief respite back in the valley when their Richmond radio contract ended (they lived temporarily with Maybelle's brother and his family because Eck had sold the home place, according to Zwonitzer), they headed to Knoxville, Tennessee, to perform on WNOX radio's popular show *Midday Merry-Go-Round*.

In Knoxville they met and, if it can be said this way, *married* Chester Atkins, better known as Chet. The shy but gifted guitar player was a part of the Carters' lives ever after. Mom described him as "closer to us than a brother. . . . There is no way I can ever tell you what Chester meant to me and all of us and how much he taught us. . . . He is one of the greatest guitar players in the world, and he was part of our family. He added to our lives and our show, and the quality of our music improved."[12]

I have listened to the recordings of those early performances in Richmond and in Knoxville. Mom is prominent in the music, maybe singing a bit out of tune, but always in perfect time. The backing music of Chet and Maybelle is undeniably brilliant. Looking back now, seeing how Maybelle and Chet played together and knowing their influence on music in the twentieth century and beyond, it seems obvious that this little band of unlikely characters was undoubtedly one of the greatest in the history of modern country music.

But they were more than just a band. They were a family, and like Mom said, Chet was part of it. So when the Carters were invited to move to Springfield, Missouri, to perform on KWTO radio, of course they insisted that Chet, as well as his wife, Leona, and daughter, Merle, come too.

Mom wrote that their big Cadillac was packed with the five Carters plus Anita's big bass fiddle taking up most of the backseat where the girls practiced their parts as the miles rolled by. More times than not, Maybelle was at the wheel, and while she was known for her calm, laid-back demeanor everywhere else, when it came to driving, she apparently was like a woman possessed. According to everything I've heard, she *flew* over those roads, pedal to the floor. And so did Eck, when he was driving. Most family storytellers agree, though, that if their passengers had a choice, they'd choose to ride with Maybelle rather than the easily distracted Eck.

The Carters moved to Springfield because KWTO produced dozens of live and recorded music shows each week for broadcast; it also distributed syndicated copies of many of its recorded shows and sent groups of musicians touring around the region to perform shows—promoting music in tiny school gymnasiums and barnlike auditoriums. Eck considered it a wise business decision, although by now his daughters had reached the age where they didn't always agree to his plans without some negotiating and/or complaining.

The move to Springfield caused Anita to drop out of high school. And for Helen, it meant a separation from Glenn Jones, the boy she'd fallen in love with back in Richmond. Most members of the family suspected that breaking up the romance was Eck's ulterior motive in moving the family to

Missouri, but if that was the case, it wasn't long before his plan failed. Glenn showed up in Springfield shortly after the Carters arrived, and he and Helen were married there a few weeks later. Helen promised she would continue singing with her musical family, and she did. But the Carters didn't stay in Springfield much longer.

By 1950, they were in Nashville.

The Grand Ole Opry had been in existence since November 1925, when radio station WSM originated a country-music program called the *WSM Barn Dance.* In 1927 George D. Hay, the show's founder and also WSM's program director, renamed it the *Grand Ole Opry.* By the time the Carters received their first invitation to join the Opry, it was the largest live country radio show in the nation.

Ezra turned down the offer.

They wanted to go, of course. There wasn't a country-music performer in the country who didn't. The problem was that the Opry's offer came with one condition: only Maybelle and the girls were invited; Chet Atkins could not come.

The musicians who worked at the Opry back then were also Nashville's premier studio musicians. Their fear was simple: if a guitarist as talented as Chet came to town, he would take away all their work. He was that good.

Ezra listened to the offer and gave the Opry a flat no-thank-you. He would not budge on his principles. Either Chet came with Maybelle and the girls, or they didn't come at all.

At the time, it was absolutely unheard-of for a country group to turn down the offer of a steady job at the Grand Ole Opry. There must have been lots of raised eyebrows, whispered mutterings, and unspoken astonishment when Ezra's answer came in. *Imagine. A country group turning down an invitation from the Opry!*

But Ezra stood his ground, with his family standing in agreement beside him. And before long, the Opry gave in and allowed Chet to come along.

The requirement, Mom said, was that Chet couldn't work with anyone except Maybelle and the Carter Sisters for the first six months.

Of course, history would show that, to a certain degree, those Opry musicians' fears were well founded. Chet did, in essence, take over the Nashville studio scene. However, with his gentle charm and endearing demeanor, he became an added treasure, rather than an intrusion. He went on to be one of the most beloved, successful, and influential producers and guitarists of all time.

Chet always credited Maybelle as his greatest influence. In *Will You Miss Me When I'm Gone?* Mark Zwonitzer says, "In later years, [Chet] minced no words in expressing his gratitude. 'I owe everything to the Carters. . . . I don't know what . . . would have happened to me if I hadn't run into 'em.'"[13]

And musicians weren't the only ones the Carters helped. In May 1952, a school bus crowded with high school seniors arrived in Nashville after a two-day drive from the tiny Ozarks town of Gainesville, Missouri, where the Carters had performed in the school gym under the auspices of KWTO. But when the bus stopped in front of Ryman Auditorium, the students were dumbfounded to find a big sign that said, "Sold Out for Six Weeks."

Undaunted, class sponsor Larry Clark hopped off the bus and made calls back to Missouri until he found someone who knew the Carters from their days on KWTO's "Ozark Jubilee" show. He eventually got the phone number for June Carter and, as he says, "just called her up." Mom somehow got tickets for everyone, even the bus driver. "Twelve rows back from the stage," one of the class members recalled, still marveling at what happened.

Mother Maybelle and the Carter Sisters had reached the top of the ladder. They were regulars on the Grand Ole Opry. What a rush that must have been for these plainspoken people from the mountains, what a sense of accomplishment they must have felt. And yet . . .

Something was missing. Mom told about the thrill of "performing every Saturday night at the Ryman Auditorium along with Hank Snow,

Roy Acuff, Minnie Pearl, Hank Williams, Faron Young, Carl Smith, Webb Pierce, Uncle Dave Macon, Ernest Tubb, and Red Foley." But somehow, it wasn't enough.

"Sometimes at night I would cry," she admitted. "I had fulfilled my ambition to be an entertainer, but somewhere inside there was still an emptiness. I didn't know what I was crying for."[14]

FOUR

Opry Star

When I woke from my dreaming,
Idols were clay,
Portions of love then
Had all flown away.

— A. P. CARTER
"Wildwood Flower"
Recorded by
the Original Carter Family,
May 10, 1928

Mom brought her unique comedy and down-home charm to the Opry and to the assorted other venues where she and her mother and sisters performed. Helen had left the group to stay home and have babies, and the Carters had hired multitalented Becky Bowman of Kansas City to take her place.

June and the rest of the Carters loved Becky, and as they had done with Chet, they immediately adopted her into the family. Mom described her as "my dear friend for life and my sister in Christ."

It was the custom then that Opry acts would take to the road during the week. Mom described those days as a whirlwind of riding and performing.

People often saw those Carter girls driving through the country in that long Lincoln with the windows open—Becky wearing her long-billed cap supporting a cold, wet washcloth dangling in front of her nose cooling her face as the wind passed through it—driving after a Saturday night perform-ance to make another show date somewhere in Pennsylvania, Arkansas, or Texas. It was nothing to drive eight hundred miles during the night and play three to five shows the next day in an old vaudeville theater.

But I don't remember my mother ever complaining. I always wondered how she did it.

Mom's skits, though undeniably silly, were also creative. They quickly endeared her to the crowds. For example, she always loved to joke about bathing suits . . .

My boyfriend gave me a new bathing suit—
Well, actually, it was just a bottle of suntan lotion and a zipper.

I was gonna be in the Miss Universe pageant. I got me one of them backless,
strapless, bottomless, topless bathing suits to wear in it . . . then they found
out it was just a belt.

She would sometimes warn the girls in the audience to watch out for the boys in the band:

Wilbur, there, is wearing a new aftershave. It's called, Come and Get It.
And I'm wearing some new perfume called, I Wouldn't Know What I'd Do
with It If I Got It.

She loved to make up funny poems. Here's one she called "the world's shortest poem about the world's first fleas":

Adam

Had 'em.

She might jokingly suggest a song to the boys in the band like "He Was Tall in the Saddle . . . 'Til He Busted His Blister." Before she started to sing, she would invite her fellow pickers to "move in close." Then she might say, "We'll all start together. Then, after we get started, it's every man for his-self 'til we get through this thing."

Back at the Opry on Saturday nights, she sang comical songs and joked with Roy Acuff and Minnie Pearl. Her country-girl act was appealing and funny, and audiences loved it.

Mom's wit and style charmed not only her audiences, but also her fellow performers. Although I never heard her put it this way herself, Zwonitzer says she "had become one of the most popular stars in Nashville and had a long line of suitors."[1]

In 1952, the year she turned twenty-three, she married Carl Smith, a young, dark-haired Opry star. They bought a home on acreage in Madison, Tennessee, a few miles north of Nashville.

Theirs would seem like the consummate country-music love story— two big-name Nashville stars fall in love, marry, and move to a pretty home in (where else?) the country to live happily ever after. But there were troubles early on. Mom was a Nashville star, but she still longed for some-thing more. She was thinking about going into acting, maybe doing tele-vision or films. Her big dreams seemed to leave her no choice but to follow her heart.

Although Carl had attracted his own legion of female "suitors"—at least he did before they were married—Mom never seemed to accuse him of causing their breakup; instead, she put the blame on herself. In *Among My Klediments*, she devotes only one paragraph to the end of their marriage:

There is no way to put a finger on why that marriage failed. Perhaps if I had remembered all God's promises and claimed them in my life, it would have been different. God's order to wives is an important part of a successful marriage, and I'm afraid I fell short of what a wife should be. I continued to work with my mother and sisters. Carl was going one way, and I was going another. If a wife expects to keep her husband, she must think first of God's order—be a helpmate and forsake mother and father.[2]

Carl may have wanted a more stay-at-home wife, someone who was not in the limelight as much as he was. Whatever caused the problems, by the time their baby, Rebecca Carlene (named after Becky Bowman and the baby's father, Carl), was born in September 1955, Carl had already moved out of the Madison house. Their divorce was finalized the following year.

June was heartbroken when Carl left her. Yet she didn't sit home and grieve. "When your heart's broken, you gather the pieces together, take your little girl, and catch a plane to New York City," she wrote. "When I went to New York, I thought I was the ugliest girl who ever lived. You feel that way when a marriage fails."[3]

Back in 1949, Mom had been invited to New York by record producer Steve Sholes. She went to the big city, accompanied by her dad, and recorded some songs and did some work with the comedy duo Homer and Jethro. With them she recorded a parody of "Baby, It's Cold Outside," a pop hit tune at the time, and "Plain Old Country Girl."

I can't help but think that first trip to New York forever influenced her life. She saw the fashion, the style, the opportunities, the money, and the education the city offered. When her marriage to Carl Smith ended, she felt New York beckoning her. *Come here and recover,* the city seemed to say to her. *Come here and change. Make a clean break. Begin again.*

First cousin Ester Moore said Mom told her, when she left for New York, "I'll always move forward. I'll never go backward. And I will never be poor."

With that determination firmly in place, in late 1955 or early 1956 she moved to New York with baby Carlene to attend acting school. She studied with Sandy Meisner, a drama coach who'd been recommended to her by Elia Kazan. Mom eventually moved into an apartment on East Sixty-Seventh Street. She liked to say that her bright young friend Rosemary Edelman, a fellow drama student, came to spend the night one time and stayed two years. Rosemary said later, "This wonderful lady wrapped her arms around me and said, 'You're mine!'"

Surely no two roommates ever had such different backgrounds: a Christian single mom from the mountains of southwestern Virginia and a Jewish girl from California. They learned from each other and enjoyed big-city life. Mom said she thought her roommate was "a pauper"—until she met Rosemary's family the next year when she went to Hollywood to do some work. Only then did she learn that Rosemary's father was Louis F. Edelman, a top-name producer in television and films.

In New York, Mom studied hard and "pounded the pavement," as she would say, seeking roles. Part of the time she was in the city, Carlene stayed back home with Mother Maybelle. Other times, Carlene was in New York with Mom. Most weekends, Mom said, she flew back to Nashville to work at the Opry and let Carl see the baby, then she would return to the city— unless she was running out of money. Then she might stay home another week to work a few shows before heading back to the city.

She got some roles in films and occasionally guest-starred on various television series. She enjoyed the work, but it didn't develop into anything special until many years later, when she played the mother of her longtime friend Robert Duvall in his highly acclaimed film *The Apostle*. Mom had attended acting school with Robert during her time studying in New York.

Mom dreamed of being a big-screen actress, and she did well in the parts she played. But her greater talents were obviously elsewhere, as a stage performer and spontaneous comedian.

In 1957, she and Carlene moved back to Nashville from New York, and soon, suitors and courtiers once again surrounded her and gave her plenty of attention. One of these beaux was another dark-haired southern boy with an emerging singing career. Throughout my life, I would see Mom get a mischievous twinkle in her eyes whenever she mentioned Elvis Presley. Her eyes would flash merrily, and she would say, "You know, son, your father was always jealous of Elvis." She even told me once that she sometimes wondered what would have happened if she had fallen in love with Elvis.

Mom and Elvis occasionally toured together, along with other performers, sometimes including Mother Maybelle and one or more of June's sisters. The Carters were friends with Elvis, and there are stories about Mother Maybelle sewing buttons on Elvis's shirts when they popped off during his wild onstage gyrations.

One time Mom laughingly showed me a billboard poster of her first husband, Carl, on which Elvis had drawn an ugly mustache and ridiculous glasses. Below the picture was scribbled, in Elvis's handwriting, "Painting by Presley."

Though Mom always maintained that she did not have an affair with Elvis, Carl seems to have believed differently—and perhaps for good reason. After Carl moved out of their Madison home, Mom would sometimes let Elvis stay at the house to "rest" after a tour.

Like most children, when I was young I thought my mother was capable of doing no wrong; I was confident that she was pure and without blemish. This is not—and was not—true, of course; no one is perfect. I know a lot more about my mother now than I did when I was a boy. But I also know without a doubt that she was a good person of high standards and solid morals. On the other hand, she was being charmed by one of the greatest sex symbols of our time. The temptation to give in to his advances, at least in some small way, would have been tremendous. I have a hard time blaming her.

Sometimes when she went out on the road, the touring group included another dark-haired, good-looking man who was also attracted to her. In fact, he had admired her since childhood when he had listened to her singing with her mother and sisters on the radio. She had met him backstage at the Opry in the mid-fifties and, even though they both were married to other people then, he had reportedly told her he was going to marry her someday. Her reply was said to be, "Good. I can't wait."

This young star's fans always roared when he stepped onto the stage and said, "Hello, I'm Johnny Cash." But his family and friends called him John or J.R.

There were lots of handsome young men to choose from out there in the music world. Interestingly, the man Mom married the year after she returned from New York had little or nothing to do with music. Rip Nix was a stockcar driver and ex-football player—"a fine young man," Mom said, from right there in Madison.

They were married in 1957, and their daughter Rozanna Lea—always known as Rosey—was born the next year. Rip moved into Mom's house in Madison, and from all outward appearances, theirs was a happy and strong family.

"I never saw Mom and Rip fight," my sister Carlene told me. "Mom kept the house extremely clean . . . to the point of near obsession, really. We all had our chores, and Rosey and I always felt loved and cherished. On the other hand, I never saw Mom and Rip give each other any open affection."

Mom continued to work and was often on tour with Johnny Cash or other headliners, leaving the two girls in the care of Rip and a nanny.

"Mom was gone a lot," said Carlene. "She was always on the road—often with 'Big John'—and the money was good. We stayed home with Rip and the nanny; however, Rip was hardly ever there when Mom was traveling.

We also spent a lot of time with Maybelle and Ezra." Our grandparents, the elder Carters, had settled not far away from Mom's Madison home.

Some of Carlene's favorite memories were the times "when we went on the road with Mom and John. He was on drugs fairly heavy then, but Mom would never let us see his addiction close-up. She kept us away from him if he was stoned."

Mom's second marriage gets an even shorter mention than her first in her book *Among My Klediments*. She wrote, "We tried hard to have a good marriage. But it seemed Rip and I came from two different worlds. After six years, that marriage ended in divorce."[4]

Carlene said she and Rosey "never saw the end of Mom and Rip's marriage coming. Mom simply put Rosey and myself in the car one time when she headed out on the road to join Johnny. She said, 'Girls, when we come home this time, Daddy Rip won't be living here anymore,'" Carlene said. "I really do not know what happened, exactly. The flame of their love was undeniably out for some time, but we never saw them fight, not even once."

Rosey always told a different story. She described a more difficult childhood, hinting about times she would not speak of—hard times at home. But Rosey was always prone to exaggerate, and in fact was a chronic liar.

The facts are that, for whatever reason, the marriage ended and Rip moved out. Mom described that time as "probably the lowest point in my life." She was ashamed to have had two failed marriages in a time when divorce was almost scandalous. "I couldn't hold my head up and look people in the face," she wrote. "I was so ashamed at having gotten a second divorce that I kept it a secret for a long time. My parents didn't even know Rip and I were separated until he'd been gone for two months."[5]

It was a hard time, and once again Mom pulled herself through it by focusing on her career. More and more that career became entwined with the career of Johnny Cash. Soon it was more than their music that brought them together. Soon their love for each other would change everything.

FIVE

When Hearts Like Ours Meet

The taste of love is sweet
When hearts like ours meet.
I fell for you like a child,
Oh, but the fire went wild.

—JUNE CARTER AND
MERLE KILGORE
"Ring of Fire"
Recorded by Johnny Cash, 1963

On December 7, 1961, at the Big D Jamboree in Dallas, Mom had made her first appearance ever as a regular part of the Johnny Cash Show. Their joint billing worked very well. June Carter and Johnny Cash had a great stage charisma together.

But Mom was at first reluctant to join him as a regular member of the tour, because she'd learned that Dad had a drug problem, and he had already become known as quite a live wire. As Steve Turner wrote in *The Man Called Cash*, "The Cash entourage developed the art of hotel destruction, something that fell somewhere between outright vandalism and an elaborate practical joke."[1]

Their redecorating tools included everything from fireworks and starter guns to paint and saws. Dad had smashed antique chandeliers in a Vancouver hotel and had been arrested for kicking down a nightclub door in Nashville. In 1965 he was banned from the Grand Ole Opry after kicking out the stage lights.

Dad told me a story of how they once pulled into a small Midwest town early one Sunday morning, having driven all night long. They were in the habit at the time of carrying a chainsaw in the trunk, just in case they wanted to make a connecting hotel suite where there wasn't one. They saw a medium-sized oak tree in a perfectly manicured lawn that morning, surely a prized tree because it was the only one growing in the yard. The boys pulled over, got out of the car, started up the chainsaw, and cut down the tree. Then they drove away quickly before anyone came out to investigate. It was such senseless destruction—and just plain mean. Those guys wrote the book on the rock-and-roll road life, which was greatly imitated but probably unsurpassed by those to follow in their footsteps.

Mom surely was wondering if she was ready to be a regular traveling companion for such a wild man, but finally Dad made her an offer she had trouble refusing: he would pay her a monthly salary, based on the number of shows he performed, and if for some reason she could not make a show, he would pay her anyway. She accepted his offer, and from then until their retirement in 1997, she was a part of the Johnny Cash Show.

I know my mother enjoyed her early years on the road with Dad, because she told me about them often. But I also know there had to be many trying times as well. For starters, they fell in love while they were both married to other people.

Dad's home life, in particular, was a mess. Although he had married Vivian Liberto in 1954, and she and their four daughters were living in California, he rarely visited. And when he did, things were troublesome. Over the years, their marriage, like June's two, had disintegrated, and by 1965, he was asking Vivian for a divorce. At first she refused. Vivian was a devout Catholic, and at the time, the church was simply not granting divorces. But by 1966, she'd had enough. It took awhile to work through the stormy settlement, but the divorce was finalized on January 3, 1968.

In *The Man Called Cash*, Steve Turner tells of my sister Kathy asking her mother how the divorce would change things: "Vivian told her that she shouldn't worry too much, because the only difference would be that Daddy's clothes would no longer be hanging in the closet."[2]

Dad had been staying with a friend, Gene Ferguson, in Brentwood, a suburb of Nashville. As the divorce proceedings were wrapping up, he moved into a one-bedroom apartment in Madison, north of Nashville. The apartment was close to the home of Maybelle and Eck Carter, who had become his steadfast friends over the years as the Carters performed with him, and it was also close to June's house. He hoped that his relationship with her would turn into more than friendship, and I am quite certain that he moved to Madison primarily to be close to her.

Waylon Jennings moved into the apartment with him, and the place must have become a real dive with the two drug-addicted bachelors coming and going whenever they weren't on the road. Fortunately, Dad didn't stay there long. He soon bought a large house overlooking Old Hickory Lake in Hendersonville. The house was about twenty miles north of Nashville and still not far from June and her parents.

He was ready to make a fresh start, give up drugs, and become a family man, with my mother at his side. But how would he find the strength he needed to achieve those goals?

Dad always carried his feelings on his sleeve, and those were very difficult times for him. One thing I feel the film *Walk the Line* lacked was a strong depiction of his loneliness during this time, his sense of isolation, and his internal struggles. Those struggles within him were surely his greatest challenge of all.

Mom and Marshall Grant, one of the members of the Tennessee Three, the band that was traveling with Dad at the time, took on the caretakers' role when they were on the road. Mom pressed his shirts, made sure he was eating, and made excuses for Dad on stage when he was late for performances. Sometimes she and the band and the others on the tour would play the full show without him, nervously trying to appease the crowd that had come to see Johnny Cash.

In *The Man Called Cash*, Marshall Grant described Dad's two polar-opposite personalities during this time:

> John R. Cash was one of the greatest human beings who ever walked on the face of this earth. But Johnny Cash was probably the greatest jerk that ever lived. He had become two different people. That's the way it was. You can't explain it any other way. He was one of the kindest human beings you could imagine and then something would trigger him and he'd come back in the room a totally different person. It would be a 180-degree change.[3]

Mom wrote in her book *Among My Klediments* that she had first caught Dad popping pills at a show in Macon, Georgia (probably in 1962). It scared her to death; she described her discovery as "a terrible shock." She and her family had become close to Hank Williams in the 1950s, and she had seen firsthand what drug addiction could do to a person. She didn't want to relive that experience again.

I do know that, early on, she hunted for his pills while he was asleep or passed out and then flushed them down the commode. She once told me that if she had a dollar for every pill of Johnny Cash's that she'd flushed, none of us would ever have to work again. Mom continually strived to get Dad off the pills, and while she did so, she basically carried the road show during the 1960s and beyond. She loved him, and she wanted him to succeed—and most of all, to survive.

Dad would promise again and again to kick his habit, but the demons inside him eventually overpowered his good intentions. Heartbroken by what was happening, Mom was, above all, trying to save Dad from himself. She wrote, "I begged, cried, demanded, hollered, prayed, humbled myself in front of God. He was the only help, because Johnny Cash sure was hooked, and I wanted so for him to be well. . . . But his only drive seemed to be to get more pills. . . . There are so many things I could tell about those years . . . the wrecks, the pain, the hurt. He should have died a thousand times from an overdose or a wreck. . . . But God never let him go, and neither did I."[4]

Surely there were several factors to my father's straightening up and becoming sound in the late sixties, including my mother's great love and support. However, I believe the greatest change occurred when he finally faced his demons, alone.

It happened when he went into a cave on the land he had bought near Chattanooga close to the Tennessee River. He went in alone, but I believe he came out with God. He got lost in that cave, perhaps deliberately, and nearly died. Mom had told him at the time she would not work with him or be with him in any way until he straightened up and got off the drugs. I believe he decided to give up, crawl into that cave, and die. He said he took a guitar into the cave with him, set it down, and never found it again.

Somewhere in the darkness of that chilling cavern, though, in fear and desperation, he found something else: the strength to change his heart. He made a promise to himself and to God: he would find his way out of the darkness and begin a new life.

That cave is now underwater, forever unreachable, its secrets flooded into oblivion with the rising waters of Nickajack Lake, which was impounded in 1967.

He returned to Hendersonville and holed up in his new lake house to get straight. Many people helped Dad through a myriad of ordeals and recoveries during his life. But according to my Aunt Reba Cash Hancock, Dad's sister, this particular recovery was a solitary thing.

Not that he totally withdrew from those around him. Mom took him to church during that time, and he renewed his relationship with Christ. When he had straightened himself up, early in 1968, she let herself fall deeper in love with him. And his love for her grew even stronger. Without Mom's love and support, Dad knew he never would have found the strength he needed to put his life in order. He acknowledged that fact often.

With his divorce from Vivian finalized and his body finally free of drugs, all obstacles seemed to have disappeared. The only thing left to do was pop the question . . .

On February 22, 1968, while performing on stage in London, Ontario, Canada, in front of thousands of fans in the audience, Dad asked my mother to marry him.

She described that night to Johnny Carson on the *Tonight Show:*

Johnny Cash straightened himself up, really, and he proposed to me on the stage in front of about seven thousand people in London, Ontario, Canada. . . . Scared me to death. I kept saying, "Shut up." And my mother was there and my sisters and the Statler Brothers, and they kept laughing at me and I couldn't say anything. I didn't know what to say. And he just stood there and looked at me and grinned until I said something. I said yes.

SIX

Mrs. Johnny Cash

Her love filled every room he was in, lighted every path he walked, and her devotion created a sacred, exhilarating place for them to live out their married life.

— ROSANNE CASH
May 18, 2003,
describing June's thirty-five-year
marriage to Johnny Cash

Dad's big proposal came toward the end of February 1968, but he and Mom agreed to wait until summer to get married so Mom's daughters, Carlene and Rosey, wouldn't have to change schools in the middle of the year.

The girls had other ideas.

"Mom and John came to us and told us they were going to get married," my sister Carlene recalls. "But they said they were going to wait until June."

How the girls knew the difference in marriage laws between Kentucky and Tennessee, I'll never know, but according to Mom's version of the story, Carlene and Rosey listened to their plans and answered, "Why wait? You could get married in Franklin, Kentucky, in three days."

And so they did. On March 1, 1968, Valerie June Carter became Mrs. Johnny Cash.

They were married in a small church in Franklin, Kentucky, by Reverend Leslie Chapman with Mom's girls serving as bridesmaids. Dad's best man was Merle Kilgore, an old friend of both my parents and co-writer with Mom of "Ring of Fire." Family friend Micki Brooks was maid of honor.

My mother beams in the wedding photo, and Dad appears thoughtful and content.

Courtesy of House of Cash

Wedding day, March 1, 1968, in Franklin, Kentucky.

A few days later, there was a big reception at the lake house with all their friends and family members gathered. Grandpa Eck and Grandma Maybelle were there, of course. In *Will You Miss Me When I'm Gone?* Mark Zwonitzer suggests that Eck "beamed with triumph" seeing the match he'd hoped for.

Mom had not changed her professional name when she married Carl Smith or Rip Nix, but on that day in 1968, she made a decision for the rest of her life. She changed her stage name to June Carter Cash.

Mom and Dad were married on a Friday, and the girls enrolled in school in Hendersonville on Monday. "We all moved directly into the house with John after the wedding," said Carlene.

Right away, things were different. Mom was different too.

"At our old home, Rosey and I had chores," Carlene said. "We mowed the lawn, did the dishes, dusted, and vacuumed. When we moved in with Big John those chores stopped. "We had people cleaning up for us hand and foot," Carlene said. "Mom said now that we had a full-time staff and lawn workers, life would be different."

I must confess that I was treated the same when I came along a couple of years later. As a child, I was always looked after and waited on hand and foot, as Carlene said. I didn't learn how to clean or do laundry until I moved out on my own at age eighteen. All of us kids were spoiled, and the truth is, I was spoiled most of all. (I'm sure you're surprised to read that, right?)

Mom changed considerably in some ways when she married Dad. Carlene said Mom had had quite an obsession with neatness until they moved in with Dad. Then she didn't enforce that neatness so strictly anymore. Mom wrote, "I am a good housekeeper, but I also think sometimes you have to live with good clean dirt."[1]

She loved being Dad's wife, and she was usually ready for just about anything he wanted to do. She said he once told her that twenty-four people would be coming for lunch. Instead, seventy-six showed up. Mom just laughed and made do. She had several freezers and several sets of china, and she could put on a spread like no one else.

Although Dad had indulged in some wild behavior as a young music star traveling the world, he came to share Mom's attitude that with fame a certain responsibility takes hold. I'm certainly not saying that Dad didn't give in to more wild behavior after he married Mom, but her gentle, patient influence on him was obvious. Her life was founded on her rock-solid Christian faith, and it was impossible to be around her and not sense that strong connection.

She also felt confident in God's grace, and she knew she had been forgiven for her own past diversions off the narrow path. She said sometimes people would question how she could claim to be a Christian when she had two failed marriages, two divorces behind her. Her answer came quickly: she had surrounded herself with the forgiving grace of her Creator, the love and promises of Jesus, she would say, and she knew she was a beloved child of God. Case closed.

As Christians, she and Dad believed the most important thing they could do was to spread the gospel. Not that Dad didn't give in many times to drugs and craziness after his return to the church, but in publicly obvious or subtler ways, he and Mom let it be known they were believers.

The Johnny Cash Show aired on ABC television from 1969 through 1971, and though it was for the most part a secular show, Dad and Mom always included gospel songs in the show's lineup. Many viewers had written letters asking, according to Turner in *The Man Called Cash*, "whether the gospel songs had a deeper meaning for him."[2]

In answer—and in defiance of the show's executives who warned him not to do it—Dad read a statement that described God as "the Number One most powerful force" and the devil as "Number Two."

He said, "Well, here lately I think we've made the devil pretty mad because on our show we've been mentioning God's name. . . . Well, this probably made the devil pretty mad all right, and he may be coming after me again, but I'll be ready for him. In the meantime, while he's coming, I'd like to get in one more lick for Number One."

Mom and Dad wanted the world to know they had fallen, they had struggled, yet their faith was as strong as ever. Some said that Dad's televised statement had a disastrous effect on the show. The series ended shortly after that. But it certainly didn't keep Mom and Dad from continuing to proclaim their faith.

In the 1970s they developed a close relationship with Billy and Ruth Graham, who became their steadfast friends. Though they sometimes went for long periods of time without seeing each other, they corresponded regularly. In my mother's belongings, we have found many letters from Ruth. She and Mom sought each other out and made it their business to understand and support each other. To me, there are no two more loving and humble people than Billy and Ruth Graham. I will love them the rest of my life.

During my recent visit to Montreat, the Grahams' home in the mountains of North Carolina, Ruth remembered Mom's "dedicated spirit in study to the Bible and, first of all, to Christ." She called Mom "one of my dearest friends," and she shared a special memory of a time when she was in the hospital, quite ill, and awoke to find Mom "by my bedside, on her knees in prayer. I will neve forget that," Ruth said. "She showed such great love."

Another wife Mom felt close to was Lisa Kristofferson, Kris's wife, who told me that twenty-some years ago, Mom "put her arm through my right elbow when I was in a funk and whispered, 'Honey, our husbands just aren't normal!' She laughed and laughed . . . . and in that single line she changed my perspective in life."

My parents had a strong community of friends, both in and out of the music business. One of those friends, Loretta Lynn, still laughs about how people got her and Mom mixed up. Loretta told me, "I never cared, but was so proud, 'cause of my love for June and how beautiful she always was."

Loretta said she once got upset that a music magazine had run her picture without permission. "I was tellin' Teddy [Wilburn] about it and he told me to look closer. I took a better look and realized it was June! Let me tell you, my husband Doo laughed so hard. He didn't let me live that one down for a long time."

Some of my parents' friends were musicians and artists Mom—or Dad, with Mom's urging—had helped discover or had nurtured as they made their climb up the ladder to success. The Oak Ridge Boys' Duane Allen was one; Larry Gatlin was another. So were Waylon Jennings, Marty Stuart, Joe South, Hank Williams Jr., and Kris Kristofferson. Describing her "babies," Mom wrote, "I didn't give birth to them, but they're mine, whether they like it or not. I've claimed them a long time."[3]

Mom and Dad spent a lot of time on the road with some of these unofficially adopted men and their families. Lisa Kristofferson recalls how Mom "had a unique way of making everyone feel like her very favorite friend and the most amazing person she'd ever known." Lisa also tells how Mom and Dad doted on whatever children accompanied their parents on tour: "On the road she spent her time shopping for toys and books and funny trinkets to please our kids. . . . She and John always inscribed something special to each one of them and would sit at long intervals listening to their silly antics. And once June held a special tea party for the only little girl on tour."

Many changes took place in my mother's life as a result of her becoming June Carter Cash. For one thing, she didn't have to be funny anymore. As her friend Joyce Trayweek said, "She could pursue more serious performance, singing and writing. Of course, she *was* still funny, though."

She and her mother and sisters had already worked on the road with Dad for years, but by 1969, she and Dad were the most successful country duo in history. Only one thing was left to make their relationship perfect: a child. My father had four girls and my mother two; all that was missing was a son.

They tried from the moment they married to conceive, but it wasn't until June of 1969 that Mom became pregnant with me. Their relationship at that point was as good as it had ever been, and their careers were soaring. The world was their stage.

It was into this life that I was born, the seemingly perfect life. When the story of Johnny and June Carter Cash has been told in brief, this is the happy ending: they had a son, and they all lived happily ever after. That seems to be the unspoken message of the film *Walk the Line*.

Of course, that's not true. In fact it's *far* from true. But through all the years ahead, the successes and failures, triumphs and heartaches, their love lasted. Both of them wrote songs and poems describing their feelings for each other. Those lyrics played out in every day of their lives together.

A cardinal sang just for me,
And I thanked him for the song.
Then the sun went slowly down the West,
And I had to move along.
These were some of the things

On which my mind and spirit feed;

But flesh and blood need flesh and blood,

And you're the one I need.

But flesh and blood need flesh and blood,

And you're the one I need.

— Johnny Cash, "Flesh and Blood,"
Billboard #1 single, December 19, 1970[4]

And I will always love you, you'll always be mine,

Forever and always till the end of time,

Till the mountains split open with the weight of the sun,

We'll rise up together . . . as one.

— June Carter Cash,
"To John"[5]

PART 2

The Mother of a Son

June with John Carter, age three, in 1973.

SEVEN

Dreams May Come

John Carter Cash had arrived, and I was so proud to be his mother.
And his father was proud, proud to have a son. Oh, thank You, God.

—JUNE CARTER CASH
Among My Klediments

My first memories of my mother are of a delicate lady with a kind voice. Mom was very protective of me. Her hands were gentle, and her touch was soothing. She always talked quite a bit, but she was bright and affectionate.

I was born on March 3, 1970, as Mom and Dad's stardom was nearing its peak, while *The Johnny Cash Show* was airing regularly on network TV. The week I was born, Dad opened the show with a slightly different form of his usual greeting: "Hello," he said into the cameras with a broad smile. "I'm John Carter Cash's daddy."

Mom reported that they received flowers, gifts, letters, and phone calls from all over the world, including from the governor and the president. Before all the hoopla died down, she said, she'd mailed out two thousand thank you notes.

My parents kept me close to them. I even slept in the same room with them throughout my younger years. When they traveled (and they did so almost continuously), I usually traveled with them. My first trip to Australia occurred the same month I turned one year old. There are thousands of photographs of my parents and me, taken all over the world. Literally, they kept me by their side day and night.

I made show appearances from my earliest days and don't remember the first time I walked on stage without being carried, but I was likely just over three. Loretta Lynn recalled that she used to baby-sit me backstage when she traveled and performed with Dad's "Johnny Cash: The Man in Black" shows. "June would be up there singin' while I watched John Carter," she said. "The minute she was done, I'd holler to her, 'Hey, June! Come and get this little brat! I was just about to whup him!'"

Soon I was joining the show. Sometimes after singing "Boy Named Sue," Dad would say, "Well, I *did* grow up and have a son, and I named him . . . John Carter Cash!" Then I would walk out and sing something with him and Mom. I remember the rush of the crowd and the exhilaration I felt, my heart swelling with my smile. Mom had taught me the words to "Will the Circle Be Unbroken?" and at an early age I began singing it at the end of the show with the rest of the family. We also sang "Daddy Sang Bass" and "The Fourth Man in the Fire." I sang these songs with my family for the first twenty-seven years of my life, and whenever I hear any of them now, I'm instantly taken back to those exciting and joy-filled days.

I was introduced to the performer's life early on, just as my mother had been, and I was intoxicated by it in some ways, probably charmed by the crowds as much or more than they were by me. I would not trade those days for anything. We were the consummate traveling musical family, close and full of love. I followed my mother's lead and sang along.

Mom was the essence of safety and love to me then, my source of well-being. She was the one unchanging constant in a world that was always changing around me from city to city, country to country.

I couldn't help but laugh fondly, rereading her book *Among My*

Klediments, where she expounded on the importance of disciplining children and wrote that although I was a "handsome little boy," I was "not too good yet to get a little paddling." Then she added, "I'll admit we do more talking than whipping, but he really minds good."[1] (I can imagine that my sisters, reading those words, must have rolled their eyes and remembered yet again how spoiled I was.)

No, with me, Mom was not much of a disciplinarian. In fact, I only remember one time when she attempted to spank me. I think I was about three years old. Who knows what I had done, I don't remember, but I committed some kind of mischief, and she told me to go find a switch.

For those who don't know (likely those who missed out on a more traditional southern upbringing), a switch is a slim green branch off a sapling: a little limb off a little tree that parents would use—or threaten to use—to spank misbehaving children. Sending the troublesome child out to find his own switch was intended to prolong the dread of the impending punishment.

That day Mom sent me out to find a green limb of just the right length and sturdiness; I was to break it off the tree and return it to her so she could give my legs a good "switchin'." But the first two switches I brought back were not long enough or sturdy enough or who knows what. This too is part of the ordeal, testing out the switch, perhaps on the parent's hand, to see if it is suitable for use. So, at least twice, I was sent back to find a better switch. A mere twig would not do.

Finally returning with a long limb I'd broken off a willow sapling, I whined to Mom with tear-filled eyes, "It looks like a little-bitty fishin' pole, Mama."

She broke down laughing, picked me up in her arms, and let the fishin' pole switch fall to the ground, unused.

Mom was always tender, always forgiving of all her children's mistakes and waywardness—at times, more so than we needed. Although I don't remember what I did that day to prompt this little incident, I'm sure that, whatever it was, I deserved that switchin'.

My parents wanted me with them, but their lifestyle and work would not allow them to take care of me alone. Mom asked Winifred Kelly, a special-duty nurse who had cared for her at Madison Hospital, to help her find a nurse who could travel with them and help them care for me. Mrs. Kelly said she would try. Instead, after some consideration, she took on the work herself, leaving her job at the hospital after twenty-one years there.

Thus Mrs. Kelly—or K, as I called her—became as much a fixture of my early life as my parents were. A strong but gentle woman, K was always there, caring for me and tending to me when my parents were working.

Later Mom and Dad also hired K's husband, George Kelly—we called him George T.—as farm keeper. They were both in their early sixties when my parents hired them, and they became my second parents, treasured and loved. When George T. died in 1997 and when K died in 2000, I grieved for them as one would mourn the passing of beloved family members— because that's what they were to me.

The Kellys, especially K, shared Mom's strong Christian faith. Mom spent much time in prayer when I was a child. I remember once seeing her looking out the window of a bus or a plane while her lips moved silently. I asked her who she was talking to and what she was saying. "To God, son," she said. "I'm talking to God."

Mom and Dad had dedicated and inspired hearts for knowledge, and they shared a great desire for spiritual wisdom. In the mid-1970s, they completed a course of study in the Bible through Christian International Bible College. In looking through their papers now, I sense their fastidious devotion and committed seeking for an intimate relationship with God. They completed the course, and both eventually earned a doctorate degree through the Bible college.

My father's study led him to develop a special interest in the ministry of the apostle Paul; in fact, Dad's first published novel, *Man in White*, was a narrative centered on Paul's conversion. Mom continued as a student of the Bible throughout my life, and her hunger for spiritual knowledge is nowhere more evident than in the study papers she completed for those courses from Christian International.

One of the things Mom said to me most often when I was little was, "Mama loves her little son." She loved to tell about the time we were driving near Lake Tahoe when I was just a toddler. She smiled and said her favorite thing to me once again, and I answered, "Son loves his little mama." I remember her telling this story many times throughout her life.

I grew up knowing without a doubt that I was loved. We all were. The fact was that I had six older half sisters, but Mom wasn't about to let anyone stick to the facts when it came to her family. She insisted there were no "halves" and "steps" in the Cash clan. I was the girls' little brother, and they were my sisters. Period. Dad's daughters, Rosanne, Kathy, Cindy, and Tara, lived in California with their mother. Mom's daughters, Carlene and Rosey, were living with Mom and Dad when I was born, but Carlene married and moved out when I was two, and Rosey did the same when I was four.

I was too young to remember much about Carlene living with us, but I have fond memories of enjoying Rosey's playful, fun-loving nature when I was young. I was sad when she left with her new husband for Kansas after they were married. I remember how Mom cried over Rosey's leaving. And I remember how concerned both parents were when reports came in of their girls' wild behavior. (I'm sure they were equally concerned when they got reports of my craziness several years later.) Their overall desire was always for all of us to be happy.

Taking Mom's cue about ignoring the facts, after Carlene and Rosey left home, and with the other four girls living in California, I quickly and comfortably moved into the role of cherished only child.

One day when Mom and Dad had gone to their Bon Aqua farm in

Hickman County, Tennessee, about seventy miles from Hendersonville, they got one of those phone calls all parents dread. It was the kind of phone call Mom and Dad would get plenty of later on as the parents of seven frequently wayward adult children. This time the call involved me, but I was only four and much too young yet to have actually caused the problem. Mom said she watched as Dad's face went white as he listened to the caller.

There had been an accident. Dad's sister, my Aunt Reba, had been driving his Jeep loaded with Carter- and Cash-family children and friends, and the Jeep had skidded around a sharp curve and flipped, throwing the passengers out of the vehicle. The others had non-life-threatening injuries, but I was trapped underneath the smoldering wreck.

A bus loaded with tourists had been driving past my parents' home when it came upon the crash site. The bus passengers managed to push the Jeep upright and lift me out of the rubble. I was completely unconscious when the ambulance arrived.

I've always been told that Dad called the police—maybe the Tennessee State Police, maybe the Nashville Metro police, maybe both—and told them he would be coming through Nashville going at least a hundred miles per hour and that if they wanted to stop him, they could follow him to the hospital and arrest him there after he had seen his son.

As they rushed to be with me, at every major intersection, Dad said, a police car was waiting, the officer standing beside his car, waving him on.

Mom always said the doctors gave me a fifty-fifty chance of surviving my injuries. I don't know whether she was exaggerating, as she sometimes tended to do, but I know the situation was serious. I was taken first to Madison Hospital then transferred to Vanderbilt. Mom said that Bob Wootton, who owned the farm near theirs, drove them into the city, and she and Dad knelt on the floorboard of the car and prayed all the way.

Quite a crowd was waiting for them at the hospital: not only family members (my sister Rosanne was there with her Bible, Mom said) and news photographers but also friends like Kris Kristofferson, Vince Matthews, Larry Gatlin, and Roy and Barbara Orbison.

I was unconscious for three days, and through it all, my parents stayed by my side. I awoke to find a black crow puppet cawing into my face and talking to me in a familiar, lilting voice. I laughed at the puppet, then at the tear-filled face of the angel behind it, my mother, obviously overjoyed to see me awake again. My full recovery was due to the doctors' good care, our family and friends' fervent prayers, and most of all, the healing power of my parents' love.

Mom wrote later that it was especially moving to be surrounded by friends and loved ones who had endured the deaths of their own children but who were still able to come to such a distressful place to comfort her and Dad. Roy Orbison had lost two sons in a fire. My Aunt Helen had lost a teenaged son in an accident. My Grandma Carrie and Grandpa Ray Cash had lost their young son (Dad's brother) Jack. Yet there they were, surrounding us with love and prayer.

Throughout my young life, Mom was a devout woman, totally committed to her husband and loyal to her home and family. She was a public figure who was always gregarious and personable with her fans. Back then, she and Dad were without fault in my eyes; they could do no wrong. I trusted completely in their love for me and their love for each other. They were everything to me. I was safe, and every piece of a happy life seemed to be in place.

Mom's support for Dad was a source of great strength and purpose for him. As Joyce Trayweek noted, "She was the woman behind the man John R. Cash. She was his strength and support." I felt completely strong and secure in their love for each other and their love and care for me. Together, we traveled the world: my father, my mother by his side on stage and off, and me.

I was totally involved with them, both emotionally and spiritually. They taught me how to pray, and they prayed the Lord's Prayer with me every night they were home. They taught me how to trust, and they instilled in me a great faith in God. I saw them pray and find purpose in their lives.

Looking back, I can see that my own faith in God was in direct proportion to my love and trust for my parents. I developed my faith through theirs. I offer this personal glimpse as a way to perhaps begin to explain my lack of faith later in life.

Those early years of my youth, I would trade for nothing. I traveled the world, met everyone from John Wayne to Richard Nixon and Anwar Sadat, and made great friends I've kept for a lifetime. Everything seemed perfect. The only life I had ever known was nothing short of a fairy tale.

I don't remember when the fairy tale disappeared and the fighting began. I don't remember what the first fights were about. But sometime in the late 1970s the problems emerged, and I got the first hints that life might not be the perfect picture I had believed it to be. Though the travels with my parents would continue, with the life experiences in many ways becoming even more profound and unforgettable, at the same time, the losses and pain that occurred would be just as defining and would carry just as big, if not a bigger, impact. The forces of addiction and mental illness would shape my world for the next twenty years.

My father was a good man in his heart, but in the late 1970s he was beginning to fall back into the throes of addiction. There were also other issues, his infidelity being one of them. He loved my mother more than life itself, but John R. Cash was an addict, and if he wasn't doing drugs, he would find a replacement for them . . .

Dad was mostly sober for the first seven years of my life. And when he was sober he was a faithful, devoted husband and a creative and inspiring father. But addiction was not something Dad would ever beat. Not in this life. And when his addiction was in control of him, he became a different person entirely.

One of the foremost qualities Mom and Dad shared was their ability to forgive and leave the pain in the past. Mom especially had the ability to heal and to forget the scars. That was her grace, her great gift to him. That is how they stayed together for thirty-five years. That is what made her a "soft-spoken woman of strength . . . strong like steel," as Joyce Trayweek says. "She was a band of steel around everyone. She held it all together."

Though Dad hurt my mother in many ways, I never saw him physically hit her. I don't believe he ever did. I was there for the worst fights and never once saw him lower a raised fist on her. I did see him raise his fist as if he would hit, but he never lowered it on her or me. No matter how out of his mind he was at the time, he remained in control, at least in this way.

One of those worst fights occurred after Mom and Dad had been arguing for a couple of hours. I had a way of inserting myself between them when they fought. I would always come into the room when they argued, then I would burst into tears and run into my room crying. This took the focus off the fight and onto me. This was my way of trying to fix them and their issues.

I don't remember my mother cursing early in my life, except for one particular fight, and it was a bad one. I remember how she screamed at my father, "I am getting the *hell out*, right now!"

This was just not something my mother would say! If Mom would say something like that, then surely their marriage was over. I thought my whole world was collapsing, and, as usual, I burst into tears in the midst of their tirade and ran to my room.

They both hurried after me to comfort me. Mom didn't leave Dad, not that time anyway. But always after that I carried a great fear with me that they would get divorced. Next to ordinary childhood worries that something would happen to them, that they would die, thinking that they might get divorced was my greatest fear.

When I was about ten, I remember being at our house in Jamaica after there had been a great tumult to strike the road show. Dad had fired several members of the band and road group, including Marshall Grant, his original bass player and longtime road manager. Jan Howard, who had been singing with the Carter Sisters for a few years, was also released. The Carter Sisters, that is to say Helen and Anita, were let go for a while themselves.

It was a hard time. And it was especially hard to see Marshall go; he had been with Dad in the early days and had worked with Dad throughout my life. He would go on to sue Dad, claiming he was an equal partner in the original Johnny Cash and the Tennessee Two (which had preceded the Tennessee Three). My feelings on this are of little importance, but I would point out that it was Johnny Cash who put the magic in their music; it was Johnny Cash the people loved. One has to ask, if not for him, would the original Tennessee Two have found success in music? Dad surely was the greater part of the trio. I don't know what was right or wrong in that situation, but I do know bitter feelings began then that remained in my father's heart for many years.

During this turbulent time, both for the touring group and for my parents in their marriage, Mom had gone to London to spend time with my sister Carlene, who had married British rocker Nick Lowe and was enjoying success in England. Mom said she needed to get away to clear her head. Unknown to me, she was considering leaving my dad.

During their brief separation I stayed in school and remained at home with K in Tennessee. I don't know what transpired between them while they were apart. But after a while, the three of us gathered at our home in Jamaica.

Colonial mansions are called "great houses" in Jamaica. Richard Barrett, poet Elizabeth Barrett Browning's great-grandfather, had built the Cinnamon Hill Great House in 1747. The ancient estate is in Rose Hall, Jamaica, just east of Montego Bay; the Caribbean Sea is in view down the mountain from the house. It is a beautiful place. My parents bought the mansion in 1973 from their good friend John Rollins. The solid English limestone structure, strong and firm, had stood for more than 250 years when my parents took the place as their own, making it into their true second home.

Elizabeth Barrett Browning's poem "How Do I Love Thee?" was one of my mother's favorites. I remember Dad giving the poem to her, written out in his own inimitable hand.

> How do I love thee? Let me count the ways.
> I love thee to the depth and breadth and height
> My soul can reach, when feeling out of sight
> For the ends of Being and ideal Grace.
> I love thee to the level of everyday's
> Most quiet need, by sun and candle-light.
> I love thee freely, as men strive for Right;
> I love thee purely, as they turn from Praise.
> I love thee with a passion put to use
> In my old griefs, and with my childhood's faith.
> I love thee with a love I seemed to lose
> With my lost saints,—I love thee with the breath,
> Smiles, tears, of all my life!—and, if God choose,
> I shall but love thee better after death.

My parents often came to Cinnamon Hill to regain their center, renew their focus. I remember how Mom danced in the yard of the estate, usually to the music within her mind. There were hundreds of birds there, and she claimed to know each one by name. She would sing and whistle to them for hours, and the birds would flutter around her, even land on her, and ride on her shoulder.

Cinnamon Hill had always been an inspiring place of healing and peace for Mom and Dad. But during this springtime break, peace seemed to have vanished. I remember sitting in their bedroom again, crying and listening to them fight for hours on end. Dad was full of pride and quick to verbally attack. Mom had had enough, and was ready to pack her bags and leave. I sat between them, tears flowing, believing that their fighting would never end . . . until they were divorced.

In the afternoon of one of these hard days, the fighting escalated to a place it had not before. Mom threatened to leave for good. Dad turned to me, sitting in my usual place between them, and said, "Son, please leave the room for a while."

I went to my room, which was next door. I could not make out their conversation through the heavy stucco walls. I don't remember how long it lasted, but eventually Dad stood in my doorway. I couldn't read the look on his face, and that scared me. He gave me an awkward little smile then said he and Mom wanted me to come talk to them. They had something important they wanted to tell me . . . together.

My heart pounded in my chest as Dad led me back into their bedroom where they had been fighting. I braced myself for what they might tell me: Their marriage was over. This family, as I knew it, was finished.

Mom sat quietly on the couch, her hands crossed on her lap. When she raised her head to look at me, she was smiling ear to ear.

Now I was *really* confused.

"Son," said Dad, "we have something to tell you."

"We're going to get married again!" Mom crowed.

EIGHT

Hostages

There stands my son. . . . He answers loud and clear, "Yes, sir." He does not move. He is very brave. The gun is still at his head. . . . Oh, Lord, help us all.

— JUNE CARTER CASH
From the Heart

It took just an instant for me to understand this unexpected turn of events, the change from hateful shouts to ardent professions of love. But when Mom's words sank in, I was ecstatic. Although I didn't fully understand the significance of my parents' desire to reaffirm their love for each other before God, witnesses, and a clergyman, it was obvious that somehow that love had been abruptly and absolutely rekindled.

I never knew what my father said to my mother that day that brought her back to him so utterly and steadfastly, but it was as if they had just fallen in love for the first time. Whatever he said and did, it was pure enchantment. Mom had forgiven him, without reservation, and their love for each other became stronger than ever.

Dad said he and Mom wanted me to be in the ceremony, which was to occur the very next day. So there was a great rush to buy a suit for me— something I'd never needed in Jamaica before.

That afternoon, a Jamaican pastor from the Mount Zion Church up the mountain presided over the event. Household staff members were the witnesses. As I recall, I gave my mother away. To be honest, the actual event has become a blur in my memory, perhaps because I was consumed with overwhelming joy and tremendous relief. My parents were as one again, and nothing would ever be strong enough to tear them apart. They were in love, and this time, nothing could stand in their way. They would be together forevermore, and their struggles were over.

I was sure of it.

I do remember the look in Mom's eyes as she vowed "I do" to my father for the second time in her life. I believe she meant it. The truth would be that her worries and pain weren't finished; this was only a brief reprieve. Yet she would hold on to that promise for the rest of her days. From that moment on, through all the uncertainty and fear that would come, her love for John R. Cash never faltered.

Mom not only loved Dad, she loved nice things—and she had a lot of them.

My parents were always free spenders and were never afraid to empty a bank account. At the same time, they were never slow to give—from their pocketbooks or their hearts. Once, I remember Mom spontaneously purchasing a purse at an upscale New York boutique. Without even looking at the price tag, she took the exquisite, soft leather bag to the counter.

The store clerk smiled at Mom with a pretentious glare. "That will be twelve thousand dollars, Mrs. Cash."

Mom didn't miss a beat. Though I saw her eyes register her surprise, she suppressed it immediately and answered, "I'll be paying with American Express," offering the woman her credit card.

It is important to mention that, despite Mom's tremendous ability to spend money, she had an excellent business acumen. Cathy Sullivan, a close family friend and business associate of my parents, said, "There might have been nothing to pass on to the next generation if June had not stepped in at critical times. She was selfless in selling precious pieces of jewelry to meet bank loans, to meet payroll, to continue the 'charity beginning at home.' She was remarkable at figuring out how to make ends meet when everyone else was falling apart. June was a good steward of the financial blessings bestowed upon her, even though she also had a 'black belt' in shopping."

I also remember quite vividly that Mom gave just as freely as she "gathered" during her shopping trips. On a New York street, I was with Mom when a homeless lady asked her for money. Always the same, no matter where she went, Mom was just as kind to that homeless lady as she was to the president's wife. That day, Mom reached into her pocketbook and pulled out a hundred-dollar bill. Smiling, she handed it to the ragtag panhandler. "Go get yourself a place to sleep and something good to eat," she said encouragingly.

She was always giving, always spontaneous, and she gave most of all to her family. Still, she did like the good things in life, including nice homes. When I was twelve, she and Dad owned a house in Port Richey, Florida; the lake house in Hendersonville; an apartment in New York City; an apartment in Asbury Park, New Jersey; the farm in Bon Aqua; and the estate in Jamaica. Each of these homes was filled with massive pieces of furniture, side tables, dressers, and cabinets, each overloaded with Mom's things. She owned more sets of fine china than most people could use in a lifetime, and she kept a great multitude of towels, linens, and silverware strewn in her many homes scattered around the Western Hemisphere.

She was a serious pack rat, and she loved collecting rarities and antiques. She had hundreds of pieces of Wedgwood crystal and various patterns of Spode china, antique Chinese pottery, and hand-painted and unique stoneware. She had a great eye for fine things, and she was always buying more, always expanding her collection.

She also had a taste for the strange and obscure. I remember for years a funny little folk-art witch riding a broom that hung on a string above her kitchen table. She had exquisite taste, certainly, but she also picked out random bizarre and weird items to fit among her fine art pieces. Her eccentricity was just part of her unique charm.

Mom did not pierce her ears until after Mother Maybelle died—not because her mother would have disapproved, but as a matter of personal choice. Up until that time, she wore clip-on costume earrings on stage. When she died, Grandma Maybelle left Mom a beautiful diamond, and Mom had it set as a gold stud earring. She had her ears pierced then and wore the earring every night of the road show, always telling the audience the story behind the beautiful diamond. She loved her jewelry as much as her beautiful household treasures.

The Jamaica house was, like our other homes, filled with treasures. In mid-December 1981, when Mom, Dad, and I went there for the Christmas holidays, I took along Doug Caldwell, one of my best school friends. Also on the trip were my Aunt Reba and her husband at the time. Cinnamon Hill Great House is up a gravel road and stands two miles off the main highway, surrounded by an expansive and stunning golf course. For a long time, my parents had maintained twenty-four-hour security at the house when we were there. But for some reason, we had stopped taking normal safety precautions. Mom and Dad had opted not to hire security for this trip, and we weren't even locking the doors at dark, as we had always done. We had developed what would prove to be a false sense of safety. The fact was, we were asking for trouble.

Four nights before Christmas, Mom and Dad hosted a beautiful holiday dinner. Aunt Reba and her spouse, Mom, Dad, Doug, and I were all gathered around the dinner table, along with Ray Fremmer, an American from Boston who had lived on the island since the 1960s. Ray was an archeologist (or a scrap-metal dealer and amateur historian, as some have called him), and he was an enormously fascinating character to me.

Ray lived thirty miles away in a dilapidated great house called Green Park. He had a comical sense of morbidity and had dug up the graves in his backyard, relocating some of the corpses buried there, but leaving some bones where they lay after excavation. His front yard was solid bedrock; he'd sold off all the topsoil. Jamaican soil is rich in valuable bauxite, and Ray had actually sold off all the soil for the bauxite to be mined from it. Dad used to joke that Ray was the only man he knew who had a yard sale—and sold his yard.

In Ray's storerooms were numerous skulls he had unearthed, both human and animal. As a child, his house fascinated me. It was the only place I knew where it was possible for the bravest visitors to descend the stairs into the underground crypt and lie down beside a skeleton. Ray had whale skulls and ancient Indian beads. His old mansion was full of dark corners and dusty rooms to explore.

Back at Cinnamon Hill on the night of the dinner party, the meal was a substantial spread. I specifically remember roast turkey, rice and beans, green beans, and fried plantains, and I'm sure there were more gastronomical delights as well. It was just past dark, and the warm trade winds were blowing through the open doors and windows of the house. This was the nicest time of day; the birds outside were quieting down, and the sun was setting, leaving a beautiful glow over the landscape.

The house staff was with us in the dining room as we all sat with heads bowed, preparing for them to sing a hymn. Mom called this "singing the prayer." Just as the first tones of the hymn sounded, a gut-wrenching voice, harsh and fearsome, shattered the peace: *"Someone is going to die here tonight!"* Then the angry voice bellowed from behind me. *"You are all mother [bleep] ing blood clots!"*

I turned to see three masked figures standing in the doorway. One held a hatchet, another had a dirty-looking little dagger, and the third man, the one doing the yelling, waved a beat-up, ugly-looking pistol.

I have spoken to several people who have lived through the kind of shocking, surreal experience we endured that night, and all of them said they responded as I did, with total denial and disbelief. I was simply unable to grasp what was happening and thought, *This can't be real. It must be a joke. Someone must have put these guys up to this. Do I know the men under those masks?*

The man with the knife grabbed my friend Doug and jerked him out of his seat while the gunman leaned into his face. "Tell them if we do not get three million dollars within the next hour, that we are going to kill you!" he screamed.

Doug repeated the words, but his voice was quivering so badly they were scarcely understandable—not that any of us needed to hear them repeated from his lips to strengthen their impact. Mom later remarked that the men must have thought Doug was me. I had bright red hair at the time, and Doug's hair was nearly black, much closer to Dad's hair color.

"We don't have that kind of money here!" Dad said, rising from his seat.

"You will give it to us now, or the boy dies! Sit down, or I kill him now!" the gunman retorted.

Dad quickly sat down. "We'll give you everything we have, but we don't have that much."

The men didn't believe Dad. The gunman jammed the pistol against my dear friend's temple. Doug whimpered and pleaded with the man, "Please believe him. He will give you everything."

The men whispered to one another for a few seconds, then the one with the gun, who was the only one to have spoken thus far, pushed Doug back into his seat. "And *you!*" he said, grabbing my arm. "Come *here.*"

He hoisted me to my feet. Now he held the gun to my head. "You tell them, now, [bleep]ing blood clot! Say you will die if they do not give us three million dollars!"

I will never forget how the hard, cold metal of the gun felt against my head, never forget the chill that sent icicles down my spine, never forget

Anita, June, and Helen Carter, c. 1937.

June, Helen, Anita, and Ezra Carter outside the Carter home in
Maces Springs, Va., c. 1934.

The Carter Family at WBJ in Charlotte, N.C., January 12, 1944 (from left:
Joe, Maybelle, A.P., Anita, Sara, June, and Helen).

June Carter, age fourteen.

The Carter Homestead,
Poor Valley, Va.

The Carter Family enjoying some time off from performing
(from left: June, Dale Potter, Anita, Ezra, Maybelle, and an
unknown friend).

A radiant young June
Carter, photo-booth
shots.

In 1952, WSM Radio had a Model T specially
painted to promote the Carter Family's performance on the Grand Ole Opry.

June with schoolmate Joyce Dobbins and her
future husband, John Trayweek, at Virginia
Beach, Va.

June performs sometime in the 1950s, prior to joining the Johnny Cash Show.

June receives her doctorate from Christian International Bible College.

Helen, Anita, Maybelle, and June backstage.

**Mother Maybelle
with her autoharp.**

**The Carter women in a rare candid
photo outside their family home in
Virginia (from left: Anita, June, Helen,
and Maybelle).**

**June and the girls hit the beach
(from left: Helen, an unknown friend, Joyce Dobbins Trayweek, and June).**

June Carter (center front) hosts a 1946 graduation party for friends from John Marshall High School.

June in an airplane with her first husband, Carl Smith, and Ernest Tubb.

June was well known for her signature jig dancing during performances with the Carter Sisters.

June Carter's life changed dramatically when she arrived
in New York City, fresh off a divorce from Carl Smith and full of hopes
and dreams for her future. This photograph hung over the bed
in Johnny Cash's bedroom until the end of his life.

how my head felt as if it might suddenly explode of its own volition before the gun had a chance to blow a hole through it instead. The hot fear in my groin and stomach, the complete and total powerlessness . . . these are memories that will never go away. They are the kind of memories that, for the rest of your life, make you check and double-check that you've locked the door at night. At that moment, however, I thought for certain the rest of my life would be quite short.

"Yes sir," I said, as calmly as I could. Then I repeated his words to my family—most definitely the hardest thing I had had to say in my short life.

Hearing my family's desperate insistence that we did not have even close to that much money, the three men had another brief conference, then the gunman sat me back down.

"*On the floor, mother[bleep]ers! Everyone!*" he shouted.

As we all quickly obeyed, I caught my father's eye. Never before had I seen such fear and helplessness in him. I was trying to be strong, but the look on his face tore deep into my heart. I could tell Dad feared we would not make it through this hellish night. I shuddered, thinking we all might die within minutes.

As we lay on the hardwood floors, silently trembling and praying, one of the bandits said they were going to take us, one at a time, all around the house and to our rooms, so we could give them all our money and valuables. We were completely at their mercy, not that they seemed to have any.

I don't remember who went first, but later Dad told me he had never been so afraid as when they took Mom. He was terrified while she was gone, but eventually she was returned to us, seemingly unscathed.

When they took me, the man with the knife was at my back. The sharp tip of the dagger pushed through my shirt and into my flesh. I remember trying not to flinch at the pain; I thought maybe he was going to push the dagger all the way into my back. Instead he pushed it into me just a bit, so

I could feel the burn of the metal. I moved forward, complying with his demands completely. He eased up with the blade.

While the gunman and the man with the knife pushed me from room to room searching for valuables, the man with the hatchet stayed in the room with the other hostages. I handed them everything I thought might have even the slightest value. I even made suggestions of ways they could carry more loot, pointing out bags and carrying cases. I answered every demand with "Yes sir" and "Please, sir" and "I only want to help you get away with as much as we have." I was trying my best to get close to their hearts, if they had hearts. I never looked at them closely, and they continued to keep their faces covered.

In one bedroom, for some reason, the man with the knife went on ahead, and I was left alone with the gunman. I kept my eyes trained on the ground. He eyed me mischievously and asked in his lilting Jamaican accent, "Have you seen my face? Could you pick me out of a group of men?"

"No!" I quickly replied. "You've kept your face well hidden."

I felt his grin beneath the mask, but still I looked away.

"Have you ever touched a gun?" he asked, almost casually.

"Yes sir," I answered.

"Would you like to touch this one?"

I felt my heart in my throat. "No, thank you."

"Are you scared?" he asked.

"Yes."

"Touch it," he insisted.

My eyes glued on the pistol he pointed at me, I carefully brought my hand toward its barrel, touched it lightly, then quickly pulled my hand away. *Will he shoot me now? Is this when it'll happen? Or is this some kind of game?*

The man with the knife came back into the room, and the three of us returned to the dining room.

We gave them all the money we had in the house—I believe Dad had around five thousand dollars in cash—and all the jewelry, including some exceedingly valuable watches, rings, and gold necklaces.

The ordeal lasted about four hours, which felt like four lifetimes. After they'd collected all the money and goods they could carry, it was clear the men were going to do something with us. They talked among themselves for a moment. I remember the only one who ever spoke directly to us all was the gunman; the other two spoke only to him, in quiet hushed tones. It was around ten o'clock when they had us all get up off the floor. They herded us down the stairs into the basement. Doug later told me this was the point when he felt sure they were going to kill all of us.

The basement of the old great house was concrete and plaster, completely below ground. It consisted of a wine cellar and a few other rooms, which had likely been used for storage, or perhaps at some time as jail cells. The doors to these rooms were thick, solid mahogany. It was into one of these damp, stale rooms that we were pushed. One of the men, the one with the hatchet, I think, seemed greatly concerned that we would starve to death in that room before anyone found us. He brought down all the food from upstairs and left it with us.

One of my last memories of the thieves is of the hatchet man taking off his mask and telling us he was sorry. I saw his face then for the first time. I will never understand why he felt it important to look at us, eye to eye. He was hungry, he said, and he could not feed his children. With that he shut the door. We heard the key turn in the old but sturdy lock.

And then there was this, a bit of humor in an otherwise terrifying experience. As soon as the door closed, Ray Fremmer began to eat. He sat on the floor, gnawing on a massive turkey leg as the rest of us watched in amazement. No one else could even think of eating anything, but Ray had lived in Jamaica a long time and had been through this type of thing before. Sadly, a number of years later, Ray would be murdered in a horribly violent act in his own great house.

In the basement room where we were imprisoned, there was a little light, but not much. The men had warned us not to try to get out until morning, but after fifteen minutes or so of silent stillness, we began to try and figure a way out of our prison. There was a massive standing mahogany coat rack in the room; the men smashed it against the wall, breaking it into jagged pieces. Then they took one of the longer pieces of the weighty wood and used it as a kind of battering ram until they broke a hole through the door. We were free.

We cautiously returned upstairs, and Mom immediately headed for the telephone, but it wasn't working. The thieves had cut the lines. Our next discovery was that my parents' car, an English Rover, was gone. We hurriedly locked the doors. Dad decided to wait until morning before walking the two miles to the main island road, rather than seeking help in the darkness and possibly encountering the bandits again. I don't think any of us slept that night except for Ray Fremmer, who seemed hardly affected by the robbery.

Later the car was found a few miles away, abandoned, and we did get a few other things back over the next few days and weeks, but not much. There are no secrets in Jamaica; the culprits were all found quickly. The armed robbery at Cinnamon Hill was a public embarrassment for the government, and the police reported to us later that the men were killed while "resisting arrest."

I don't hold the incident against Jamaica in any way; I will always love that country and its people, and I'll never stop going back there. That kind of thing could happen in Hendersonville, Tennessee, or anywhere else on earth. To be honest, I felt sorry for the men in some ways; I did see their human side, however briefly, while they were committing the crime. The hardest thing about their death was just wishing they had simply asked for help instead of resorting to violence. My parents certainly wouldn't have given the bandits all the cash and valuables they took by force that night, but without a doubt, they would have given the men *something* to help them through their hardship.

It was a common thing in Jamaica for those in need to ask directly for help. Ruth Graham remembered that when she and Billy visited my family there for the first time during the 1970s, "when a local would come to the gate asking for something—money, help, anything—June nor John ever let them go away empty handed." Ruth called Mom "as kind a person as I ever met. She never turned anyone down."

The fact that the thieves were killed for what they had done troubled me for a long time, especially in light of Mom's comment the day after the robbery. When I came downstairs that morning, I found her cooking breakfast with the ladies who worked at the house. I was stunned to see that she was wearing the diamond earring Grandma Maybelle had left her.

"Mom, you still have your earring!" I said. "How did they miss that?"

She smiled. "I gave them quite a bit of my jewelry, son, but not this one. I hid it behind the leg of the cupboard when they made me lie on the floor."

"Mom! They might have killed you if they'd found out you were hiding something!" I scolded her.

She looked at me with that wry sense of wit and charm she was so famous for, and her answer flabbergasted and stunned me. "Some things are worth my life, I guess."

NINE

Sunday Morning Comin' Down

Once I stood in the night with my head bowed low,
In the darkness as black as could be.
And my heart felt alone, and I cried, Oh Lord,
Don't hide your face from me.

— **MOSIE LISTER**
"Where No One Stands Alone"
Performed by June Carter at
The Louisiana Hayride, 1960

Throughout my childhood there were many long periods of travel. Life on the road was sometimes tedious, sometimes wonderful, and always remarkable. Mom was a professional traveler; she had grown up traveling with her mother and sisters, and they were all true road warriors. One of the secrets of their survival on the road was the medicine bag.

As my sister Carlene later remembered, "Everyone had one. When I began to travel, I got myself one. Everyone had a pill to mend everything. If you were constipated, there was a pill for that. If you were in pain, there was a pill for that. Long drive? Sleepy? There was a pill in the medicine bag to keep you awake. Exhausted and still couldn't sleep? There was a pill for that too."

My father adhered to this same mentality but took it to the next level. Meanwhile, my mother and aunts had more than enough over-the-counter and prescription pills to fix any given ailment. Everyone's big black medicine bag was filled to the top, hard to close because of the plethora of bottles crammed inside. It was a standing joke among the road group: everyone was always looking for the perfect pill, the one that would fix everything at once.

Mom and her medicine bag were always ready to go. And during my early childhood, she was always in control of herself and her life. She held steadfast to her truths and held her head high, even when Dad's addiction got ugly. She was forgiving and loving of Dad and yet very protective of me. I remember her coming to me during one of the bad times and saying that she and I would stick together no matter what.

When we were away from home, Mom and Dad always booked two rooms in the hotels we stayed in so that they had their own space and their own bathrooms but could still share a bed, if they so chose. During the early 1980s, they seldom did share a bed on the road. I was normally Dad's roommate; we always had double beds in our room.

Those were some of the worst times during his addiction . . . and thus for me. So many nights, I lay in bed listening to his labored breathing, and my heart would suddenly pound when the breathing would stop for what seemed like long periods of time. In terror, I'd wonder if he had died.

Many, many times I wanted to run into Mom's room to wake her and tell her of my fears, but I was afraid to do it. I loved my father very much, and if I woke up Mom, I knew she would come flying into the room and, upon trying to awaken him, discover that Dad was high again. I couldn't stand to see them fight.

In the summer of 1982 Dad was filming a movie in Central Georgia. It was *Murder in Coweta County*, scheduled for broadcast as a network television movie of the week. Mom had a small role in the movie also. We were staying in a hotel near the set for an extended time, and as usual, I was Dad's roommate.

One night while we were there his breathing was exceptionally bad. Each intake of breath was greatly labored and weak, as though he were fighting to pull the air into his chest. But even more frightening were the exhales. He would powerfully push all the air from his lungs, then he would *not* inhale. I nervously watched the seconds tick by on a bedside clock, sometimes waiting ten to twenty seconds before he breathed in again. I was terrified.

Suddenly Dad exhaled with one loud, harsh breath, then he lay very still. I waited in worry. *Breathe, Dad.* Twenty seconds passed . . . nothing . . . thirty seconds . . . *Should I go get Mom?* . . . forty seconds . . . fifty . . . I was beginning to panic. When he had gone a full minute without drawing in that next breath, I ran into Mom's room and found her awake.

"Dad's not breathing!" I cried.

She hurried back into our room and flipped on the light. Dad lay where I'd left him, as still as a corpse.

"John! Wake up!" she shouted, shaking him.

Nothing.

I frantically slapped my hands against his cheeks. "Dad! Wake up, Dad!"

He still didn't respond.

"We have to get him into the tub," Mom said, taking charge as she'd done in other tense situations. None that I was present for were as tense as this one, however.

Using all the strength my twelve-year-old body could muster, I helped Mom drag him into the bathroom. We rolled him into the tub and turned on the shower. Even the cold water splashing over him didn't immediately pull him out of his stupor. But after a few seconds, he began to come around. Soon he was up and stumbling into the bedroom.

Mom began to yell at him, and instead of curling up between them and crying as I usually did, this time I joined in. I had never told Dad how I felt about his drug abuse, but now I was so scared, so hurt and angry, I had to let it out.

"I can't take it anymore!" I cried, shaking my head and glaring at him angrily. "You have to stop the pills, Dad. You have to stop!"

As I said earlier, my father never hit me, but I had never talked to him this way, either. This was the one time he came close to lashing out at me. His dark, flat eyes flashed, and he clinched his huge fist.

"Go ahead," I said calmly. "I dare you."

I don't know what I would have done if he *had* hit me. I'm just glad he backed down. Later that night I went into Mom's room; I slept in the bed with her, and we cried together and tried to comfort one another. Back in the adjoining room, Dad slept on, his breathing still labored, the drugs still in control of him. Mom turned on the television, hoping it would drown out the sound of his loud, troubled breathing next door. But nothing could drown it out. In my mind, all these years later, I can hear it still. And even now, I cannot sleep with the TV on. I keep thinking I hear the labored garble of Dad's breathing beneath the television voices.

In several ways, that night of despair may have been a turning point for me during a time when I was coming of age. I was beginning to take more notice of the world around me, and I had even begun to consider that I might not be the center of the universe after all. With a clarity I hadn't had as a younger child, I started to see the struggles my parents had endured for so long.

Somewhere in my mind, the idea started forming that if I was going to avoid the kind of emotional hurt I had experienced because of Mom and Dad's frequent fighting and because of Dad's ever-intensifying drug problem, I was going to have to become calloused, shielded, constantly keeping my guard up.

But although I matured in other emotional ways, my relationship with

Mom was still almost that of a little boy. She was still my closest friend, confidant, and attendant, still a constant I never doubted. I knew I could count on her, even while Dad's life seemed to be falling apart. Her spirit provided the steadily beating rhythm that kept our family going. She was the one who praised God through everything, good and bad. At that point, Mom was still my everything.

During this part of my life we would usually be in our New York City apartment one week a month during the summers and at least one weekend a month during the winter, fall, and spring. The penthouse apartment was at Forty Central Park South, and it offered a mind-blowing view of the park thirty stories below, a postcard-worthy vista of the city skyline, and, for me, extreme loneliness.

Who could ever guess that a great and glorious city teeming with millions of people could be the loneliest place in the world? But for me, that's what it was. I had no friends to spend time with, and my days consisted of watching movies, going out to eat, or ordering in food. It was then, in only my twelfth year, that I began to taste real depression. I had trouble sleeping, and when I did, I had vivid nightmares.

Mom spent most of her days shopping or going to the dentist. All my parents' dentists at the time were in New York. That there were accomplished dentists in Tennessee never occurred to me then. I was sure that if you wanted to get your teeth worked on, you went to New York City. The fact was, the New York dentists were also Mom and Dad's friends, and dental work was a good excuse to go to the city and visit their friends, shop, and see movies.

Mom loved New York, perhaps because it brought her closer to her youth. Although she had moved to New York with baby Carlene on the rebound from her broken marriage to Carl Smith, she quickly overcame her heartache there and enjoyed the freedom and allure this place had to offer. Everything had been fresh and new to her then. Now, nearly thirty years later, she felt she had made great accomplishments, and her apartment on Central Park was a well-deserved reward for her hard work, a reminder that her dreams had come true. The country girl from Poor Valley had reached the top.

There were only a few things amiss in Mom's ivory-tower New York-penthouse life. Her adolescent son was miserable in her dream-come-true apartment. And the man she loved was not the same man she had married. He had fallen once again under the control of addiction.

Before I go any further, I would like to clarify something: although I may talk candidly about my father's addiction during this time of his life, I don't mean to imply that he became a bad or evil person. He wasn't one then, and he never became one. He was still a loving father; he still studied the Bible, talked to Billy Graham every week, and he was well aware of his shortcomings. He acknowledged that he had fallen.

In many ways, he was still present in my life: he loved to take me on fishing trips or to Central Park when we were in New York. What was different was that he was simply *not* present, emotionally and mentally, in the myriad ways he had been available to me before his addiction reappeared. Though he was still there physically, his spirit somehow changed when he was under the influence.

I never knew, when I came home from school or some other absence, what state he would be in. I always hoped he would be the active, involved, quick-to-laugh man I'd known during my childhood. But increasingly, I would come home to find him in an almost trancelike state, as though he were asleep but somehow still functioning—but barely. Slurred, slow speech; bloodshot eyes; a head that drooped—those were the characteristics that told me that drugs had seized control of my dad.

In contrast, during this stage of my life, Mom was strong and consistent. Mom's former Richmond classmate Joyce Trayweek and her husband, John, were close friends with Mom and Dad and saw what was happening.

Joyce was right when she described Mom during those years as "like a steady ship holding course, no matter how the wind blew. She never went off into hysteria or showed great fear. She was gentle and kind, always."

Bright and clear back then, Mom knew what she wanted. Most of all, she wanted a clean man in her life, a husband who could be counted on. Her love for him would never change, but the truth was, Dad was slipping away from her.

He spent much of his time with friends who were also on drugs. I never saw the happy, fun-loving side of my father's addiction, although I've been told it existed. Later in life, when I began to use drugs and alcohol myself, I occasionally partied with people who had used drugs with Dad. They spoke of how funny he was when he was high, what a laughable spirit he had when he was on drugs. I never saw that. To me, when the drugs had control of him, Dad just wasn't there. He was not the same man he had been before.

Because we had so many homes, we didn't spend a lot of time at any of them. Mom and Dad traveled the world and worked at least 150 days a year.

Sometimes I went with them, especially in my early childhood, but as I got older, whenever school was in session, I would stay home with K. This strong-hearted southern woman gradually replaced my mother as the most unvarying constant in my life during these years. I loved my parents dearly, but K was as much a parent to me during that time as Mom or Dad was.

The summer of 1983, my thirteenth year, was a time of rock bottoms and tumult, of unforgettable adventure and soul-searching confrontation in our family's inner circle. My memories of much of that time seem veiled, as if they are just beyond my grasp, hiding from view. The other day I came across an old photo album labeled "John Carter, 1983." I have K to thank for it. She made many photo albums, thoroughly documenting my youth. The pictures inside are of a happy, bright, cheerful boy surrounded by friends and people he loved.

Courtesy of Jimmy Holt. © *The Tennessean*

John Carter Cash, age three, with beloved nurse Winifred Kelly.

Those are accurate pictures. But there was also an element to my life in those days that isn't apparent in the faded snapshots. The events I lived through in my thirteenth year would forever change the way I viewed the world. In some ways, I grew up that year, while in other ways, I stopped growing for quite some time.

For years now, Mom had been consumed with Dad's addictions and illnesses. Since the early 1960s she had known he was capable of forgotten promises, deceit, and volatility. She had struggled with this man called Cash until she was physically fatigued and emotionally exhausted. She had flushed thousands of pills down the toilet, but there were always new hiding places. I can remember Mom tearing through Dad's closet and dressers, dumping out his guitar cases, looking inside the guitars themselves, searching under mattresses, and looking on top of bed canopies. There were stashes everywhere.

Dad was addicted, for the most part, to prescription drugs. During these times, he had many doctors who wrote prescriptions for him, and very few of them knew of the others. His first drug of choice at that time was some kind of pain pill: Mepergan, Percodan, or Percocet. There were many others. He never paid attention to the prescribed dosage and would often lose track of how much he had taken. As a result, it was a common occurrence for him to pass out on airplanes or stumble up to the microphone on stage.

I remember, in particular, one embarrassing review in a German newspaper. Dad had performed on a television show, and at the end of the show he got down on his knees and kissed the floor. In his well-intended but drug-impaired way, he was trying to show his appreciation for the audience, but his gesture was understandably misinterpreted. The front page read, "Johnny Cash Sick or Drunk on TV Guest Appearance."

He had become the same, both on stage and away from the spotlights—in the hotel rooms and on the tour bus, our home on wheels. He was there, physically, but the talented, alert, involved man I had known as a young child seemed gone forever.

Amazingly, Mom held him blameless, choosing to believe the good man she loved would eventually shine through. She was the most accepting person I have ever known. Of all I learned from her in my life, that was the most lasting and beautiful lesson. It was an admirable trait; however, it left her open to being mistreated and disrespected by the addicts in her life.

And the number of addicts surrounding her seemed to be steadily increasing, as not only her husband but her daughters—and eventually her son—fell victim to addiction's vicious hold.

Mom was by our side whenever one of her children was in dire straits, offering love and support to us when we were in pain. When I checked into a treatment center in 1991 for the first time, though she did not suggest I go, she was the first to offer support, along with my father. Mom got a message to me through my counselor. It arrived on a small piece of pink paper: "Your mom called. She said to 'be true to your own heart.'" She did not condemn or berate me; she simply supported me.

She was always there for her girls, too, when they were in trouble, going through struggles, or in pain. When Carlene was rushed to the hospital for emergency surgery in London, Dad rented Mom a Learjet to fly to England to be at Carlene's side. He did the same thing when Mom flew to Las Vegas to be with Rosey after she had overdosed on cocaine. Dad always took care of Mom unconditionally, just as she cared for her children. He would do anything she needed at any time.

Although we all took a turn, my sister Rosey probably caused Mom the most pain of any of her children. Rosey would regularly have vicious "tears," as my parents called them, when she would call, angry and needing money. One of the first such episodes I can remember occurred when we were in Montreux, Switzerland. My Aunt Reba was calling from the House of Cash offices back in Hendersonville.

"Rosey is here in the lobby with a gang of her friends." I could hear Aunt Reba's distant voice coming through the phone Mom held to her ear.

"Well, honey, that is where she belongs," Mom answered.

"But she's stumbling-down drunk!" said Reba. "What should I do with her? She's asking for money."

"Let me talk to her, Reba."

I could feel Mom's stress and fear. I was worried about Rosey, but more so for Mom's peace. I remember wanting to make it better for her, wanting to help Mom somehow.

There were times when Mom internalized her pain and her worry about the addicts around her to the point that she became sick herself. She wound up in the hospital suffering various illnesses and struggling with depression, probably a result of what she described to her cousin Ester Moore as living her life like a human pie: "I try to cut off a little piece for everybody," she told Ester. "I have a piece of my heart for so many people in so many different ways." But more often than giving in to illness herself, Mom coped with the stress of worry by showing a blessed ability to turn over her loved ones' sicknesses to God and let him deal with them.

I recall being on the road once and hearing her talking on the phone to a friend who was dealing with her husband's infidelity. "You've just got to lift them up, honey," Mom said with her magical charm. "Lift up your burdens to God. Don't carry them yourself. Between you and God and me, we can make it through this together."

Although Mom successfully practiced what she preached most of the time, and although she was often able to lift her problems—and her problematic loved ones—up to God for him to handle, sadly, there were also times when her burdens seemed to consume her. Sometimes they were just too heavy to lift at all. Then she took on the burden herself.

Though Rosey's addictions and ugliness caused immeasurable grief and pain, she was in many ways one of the most beautiful people I have ever known—when she was sober. She had a loving and tender heart. She was easy to be around and loved to have fun. She lived at home until I was four, and when she married and left home I was heartbroken. For most of my life, I was closer to Rosey than to any of my other sisters. We spent quite a lot of time together.

But soon after she left home, addictions took control of her life, just as they had taken over Dad's. The difference was that Rosey became addicted to marijuana and alcohol at an early age and then moved on to the strongest street drugs: heroin, cocaine, and speed. She became an addict not only early but quickly. I remember Mom's apprehensions starting not long after Rosey left home—and they were completely justified.

In predictable addict form, when Rosey was drugged up or drunk, she became a monster. She lost all moral control and would steal from and hurt the ones who loved her most. She showed a dark and hate-filled bitterness when she was on drugs or drinking. She would stop bathing and would dress in torn clothing and rags, something that was a terrible shock to Mom, who was always very clean and prided herself in looking nice, even when she was just working around the house. It was as if Rosey was rebelling against Mom's long-ago demands for cleanliness and orderliness when Rosey and Carlene were children being reared by a single mother.

I recall one day in that spring of '83 when Rosey came home, reeking of booze, staggering drunk, and fiercely aggressive. She stumbled into Mom's bathroom, probably looking for a handout from Mom—or hoping to steal something she could sell for drugs. I shadowed her, curious and troubled. Rosey was angry, as usual when she was high.

I cannot understand the anger she had for our mother; I don't know where it came from or why it continued. I tell myself the hatefulness was not really Rosey but the addict, the dark spirit within her, that held such contempt and resentment for the world and the ones who loved her most.

That day when Mom saw her, her face lit up, as it always did when one of her children came home. She said, "Oh, it's my Wildwood Rose! Come here, honey. You need a bath."

I left the room. Twenty minutes later, Rosey came out, dressed in my mother's new clean clothes and carrying a pocketbook. I am sure Mom gave her money that day.

Mom seldom donated to organized charities, claiming she gave enough to her own family to make up a tithe. She would say this in jest, but there was some truth to it. I saw this type of scene play out many times in our home. Mom was the most forgiving person I have ever known, but her repeated and unconditional forgiveness allowed those she loved the most to hurt her the deepest. Mom gave her whole heart and soul to her family, and, in some ways, she enabled them in their addictions.

Rosey considered herself cursed, and in believing so, became so. There were times when Rosey was one of my best friends, and I must freely admit, times during my own addiction when we used drugs together. But where I have, at this point in my life, taken God's grace and learned to live one day at a time, Rosey never did and had no intention of doing so. For me, the phrase *There, but for the grace of God, go I,* is more than a cliché. It is steadfast truth.

Rosey was a beautiful person. I will always believe that. But she was cap-tured by the disease of addiction, and that captivity would continue until she died at age forty-five of carbon monoxide poisoning in a converted school bus loaded with gas-powered heaters and drug paraphernalia. She was a beautiful soul, but that unique beauty and brilliance were scattered and lost in a whirlwind of chaos.

I saw my sister Carlene get to the same point, but today, she has miraculously found reprieve from this madness. I thank God every day for our freedom from this killer of addiction, and I pray that Rosey's story will help others see how easily we all could slip into its dark and deadly grip. I pray she has finally found peace.

While both Carlene's and Rosey's addictions were devastating for Mom and me to watch, the most staggering and constantly present addict in our lives during 1983 was Dad. His self-control seemed to be totally lost, and his consumption of drugs increased to ever more dangerous levels. There seemed to be no place of safety, no place to hide from the ugliness of his condition.

I was greatly humiliated when Dad was high in front of the school friends I brought home with me one day. And several times, Mom told me to pack my things so we could leave our home in Hendersonville on a moment's notice. When we were on the road, life was equally full of worry, fear, and embarrassment.

Most of my fears, and especially my anger, about Dad's behavior, I kept to myself. I loved him greatly, and he truly was my best friend. We went on amazing adventures together and had many happy times. He was a tender man, and I know without doubt that his love for me never waned. And although in those years he was usually high, he was seldom angry. In fact he showed little emotion at all during that time, unless he was arguing with Mom.

The most accurate way to describe our family's life in 1983 is simply to say I felt as if Dad just wasn't there. My true father had disappeared, and the man I knew and loved had been replaced by a stranger. What a shame to think that my mother and I would, in the years to come, like so many loved ones of addicts, become just as sick if not sicker than my father.

TEN

In the Land of the Midnight Sun

"Can I sleep in the middle?"

"No, your mother will sleep in the middle. She's a lady. You and I will each sleep on the edges in case of trouble."

"Trouble?"

"Yeah, in case there's a bear."

"A bear?"

"Yeah, a big Alaska brown bear. They're everywhere."

— JOHN AND JOHN CARTER CASH
quoted in June Carter Cash
From the Heart

Mom and Dad and I had been on the road most of that summer in 1983, and I was looking forward to the Alaska fishing trip Dad had scheduled for the three of us.

It would be my first trip to Alaska, but not my first wilderness fishing trip. Several times, my parents and I had enjoyed trips to Red's Camp on Lake Costigan, a remote hideaway in Saskatchewan. The camp was an hour's seaplane flight north of La Ronge and had no electricity—not even a generator—but the fishing was fantastic. Native guides provided for us superbly and always took us where the big northern pike and lake trout were waiting. Red's was a wonderful place, but I craved an adventure with a little more excitement, a few more challenges. I wanted something a little more treacherous. So I had talked my parents into a float trip through the Alaskan wilderness.

Mom normally accompanied Dad and me on our extended fishing explorations. She was always up for adventure and was likely to catch as many fish as either of us. I was constantly reading magazines and poring over brochures advertising fishing camps and float services in the Alaskan wilderness, and I had found what I believed to be the perfect place for a fishing adventure.

Courtesy of John Carter Cash

John Carter Cash in his waders in Alaska.

The excursion we planned was a five-day float on the Tikchik River from Nishlik Lake to the Tikchik Lake Narrows, where the Tikchik Narrows Lodge is located. It is an isolated location in remote southwest Alaska, and at the time, the lodge offered fishing and float trips from the more remote, northern lakes. That's what we would do.

The Johnny Cash Show's tour that summer had ended in Anchorage in early August, then the three of us were off to the wilderness. I was beside myself with excitement. Here I was, an adolescent boy who'd grown up amid comfort and privilege, and all I wanted to do was visit places that had neither. It was a lifelong dream coming true for me. Not that I had to beg too hard to make it happen. Mom and Dad were up for the adventure and looked forward to the trip.

I was in awe, flying my first time over the open expanse of southwest Alaska to the port town of Dillingham. There is no way to explain to someone who has never been there the raw beauty and mystic grandeur of Alaska. It is beyond description. At the airport in Dillingham we crossed the tarmac to board a five-passenger single-propeller plane, where a brawny man with bright eyes and gruff countenance greeted us. He introduced himself as Bob Curtis, the owner of Tikchik Narrows Lodge. Often he contracted with other pilots to fly his clients to their putting-in points, but Bob would fly us himself the rest of the way. As we loaded our gear, I eagerly climbed into the co-pilot's seat.

"Son, why are you sitting up there?" asked Mom, concern darkening her eyes.

"I want to look for caribou!" I answered. We had seen a smaller herd during our flight from Dillingham, but I hoped to see one of the giant herds I'd read about. I knew they migrated across the wilderness of tundra and brush.

"Oh, all right, son. But be careful, John Carter."

Mom probably said those words at least ten times a day—or more—on this trip. My family used to joke that I must have grown up thinking my full name was "Be Careful John Carter" because those were the words I heard most frequently for the first two decades of my life. Since the Jeep accident when I was a small boy, Mom and Dad had become even more protective of me than they'd been before. I had learned to accept their cautions and warnings, realizing it was a part of the way they loved me.

Somehow, even though I'd grown up in such a protective environment, I was, at the same time, quite self-sure and daring. I felt fully alive and indestructible, and I couldn't wait for this adventure to begin. I couldn't imagine that my daring attitude and thoughtless courage would prove to be a detriment on this trip.

But it did.

Dad and Mom both were probably worn out from all the rigors of traveling and performing. The fact was, none of us were in great physical shape—and we were in for a strenuous surprise.

The scenery on the flight north was stunning, and I did see the huge herd of caribou I was watching for. As we flew over the great open expanse of tundra to the north of Dillingham into the Wood-Tikchik State Park, Bob turned to me with mischievous eyes. "Do you want to fly this bird?" he queried almost nonchalantly.

"Yes I do, sir!" I answered excitedly.

"No, son! Don't do it!" Mom called out from her seat behind me. She probably was thinking that not only my life but hers and Dad's were at stake. Dad was mostly noncommittal, laughing quietly. I don't remember whether he objected to the plan, but I grabbed the wheel and Bob let go of the controls, and I was flying, just like that!

"Oh, dear. I don't like this at all!" Mom moaned.

I don't recall how long I flew the plane, but it was probably at least ten minutes. I was amazed at the feel of the controls in my hands, and I was in my glory: at the top of the world, figuratively and realistically.

Despite Mom's fears, we arrived safely at the lodge after I eventually relinquished the controls to Bob. We spent the night there then left the next morning by seaplane for the remote northern parts of the state park. Our guide, a tough and spirited redhead named Tim, had flown on ahead with provisions and our rafts to prepare for the trip. We landed on Nishlik Lake and were soon under way.

Mom and I both knew that Dad had been using drugs on the tour that led up to our arriving in the wilderness, and we assumed he had brought more drugs along with him. But Dad told me later that he was clean on our Alaska trip—although if that was true, it didn't happen by choice. Dad claimed he had run out of pills at the end of the tour and had sobered up on the float trip. If that was the case, he certainly did it the hard way, sweating through not only withdrawal but the physical hardships of strenuous exercise, which he had always loathed. I'm sure he got quite a workout on this trip, and certainly by the time it ended, he had to have been in much better shape than he'd been when it began.

There were two rafts. Tim was at the oars of the first one, with Mom and me as passengers. Dad rowed the second raft, which carried all the gear.

The first night we sat up late by the campfire and watched a bear across the river. The great beast sat on his side of the water, watching us. I'm sure he was trying to deduce whether or not we were something good to eat. Tim didn't sleep that night. He held his gun close and fed the fire. Dad, Mom, and I crawled into our tent and did our best to forget the carnivorous creature licking his chops across the river.

I don't recall anyone but me actually catching a fish, but I made up for the others. I seldom let my lure stay out of the water for long and reveled in reeling in big arctic grayling and char. Dad concentrated entirely on rowing and carefully steering his raft so that all the gear didn't get dumped in the river. He never even wet a line. Mom spent most of the trip writing in her journal, some of which she shared in her book *From the Heart* in the form of comical dialogue, including this conversation:

> "John, I'm not having a good time. I want to go home."
> "We're going. Just get into the raft. We're on our way."
> "I want to stop at the first store and telephone that little plane to pick us up."
> "Up? Up off of what?"
> "Maybe if it would fly low, I could grab a wheel."[1]

All through the float trip, while Dad rowed relentlessly and I cast my lure incessantly, Mom wrote in that journal. Lately, I read it for the first time and enjoyed the charm and humor that appear on every page. Her desire to "go home" was just a joke, and she was consistently upbeat and hopeful, a reminder that the trip brought the three of us closer than we had been in years. Dad's addictions were nearly forgotten, and Mom was persistently optimistic; she acted as if there were no problems in her life whatsoever.

The fact was, the only time Mom would ever admit to her heartache and angers was after she'd reached the point of nearly total emotional break-down. Such despair was far removed from the Alaska trip. We laughed together throughout our adventure; we enjoyed five joyful days of happy fun. There were no breakdowns. And although I nearly died, we finished the trip very much alive.

My near-death experience occurred the afternoon of our second day on the river. We had stopped for lunch on a gravel bar that edged a particu-larly fast-moving section of the stream. The river wasn't very wide there, and the raging current had dug deep into the far bank. The water was at least ten feet deep against the bank and so frigid it was painful to the touch. As always, I continued fishing while Mom, Dad, and Tim unloaded the canoes and heaved them up on the gravel bar. I was consumed by the water, continuously casting, and eager to catch those elusive fish.

When Tim first laid eyes on me the day before, prior to our taking to the river, he observed my chest-high waders and warned, "Those things are dangerous if you fall in the water. They fill up with water, and you sink to the bottom like a rock!"

I had paid him no heed (and Mom apparently hadn't heard him or she would have made me take them off). With thirteen-year-old arrogance, I knew I would be sitting in the raft most of the time, so there was no dan-ger. I had not taken off the waders except to sleep.

That day, as the others unloaded the rafts, I moved down the gravel bar to the riverbank, incessantly casting across the churning arctic torrent. I'm not sure if I just wanted to get my feet "wet" or if I stepped a bit too far into the current, but suddenly the streambed was giving way beneath me. The next thing I knew, I was in the river up to my chest, and icy fingers of the water were feeling their way down my body as the water poured into my waders. As I was being dragged down by the monstrous current, I remember looking at Mom, barely able to speak, and calling out a feeble "Help!"

Instantly, she was at the water's edge, calling frantically to me.

"Son! Hold your breath! Oh, dear Lord!" I heard her bellow.

Tim, only a few steps behind Mom, also reacted instantaneously. He jumped into the rushing current and somehow managed to pull my wet and weighted-down body from the current just before my head went under. I can't remember Dad's reaction, but I'm sure he was standing right beside Mom, watching in horror as the ordeal unfolded. Mom came as close to being hysterical as I ever saw her and later made a much bigger deal of the episode than I thought was necessary.

My own response was to put on my shorter hip waders and keep fishing, hardly missing a beat while Mom was probably trying to recover from serious heart palpitations. It wasn't until I was quite a bit older that I realized just how close to death I had been. The truth is, it's a wonder—and a mark of Tim's heroism—that I lived through the trip.

After five days of rafting the river (with ceaseless fishing by me), we came to the point where the Tikchik River emptied into the great Tikchik Lake. The lodge was still miles away, and getting there on the still waters of the lake would require arduous rowing. Dad had had about all the exercise fun he could stand at that point, so Tim, ever hardy and devoted to his work, attached Dad's raft to ours with a rope and began to row. After some thirty minutes of Tim's rowing our boat and also towing the raft containing Dad and all the gear, we saw a tiny speck approaching from the horizon.

It was a boat full of native people who had heard on the radio that Johnny

Cash and his family were floating the Tikchik. They had excitedly motored out to meet us. Tim gladly let the greeters tow us the rest of the way to the lodge, where hot drinks and dinner were soon served up. The trip had been a delightful thrill for me, but I was glad to sleep in a bed again.

Mom's laughter was one of the most familiar sounds I heard throughout each day of that wonderful trip. She was the same positive, fun-loving person she'd always been, showing again her characteristic way of letting go of past troubles and moving on. On the river Mom was constantly looking ahead and showing not the slightest hint of any resentments that might be hidden in her heart.

When we left the Alaskan wilderness, Dad was clear eyed and strong, and Mom was the same joyful and supportive mother I had known all my life. When we left the wilderness, there was still hope for the future of our family. And for a short period, I was as happy as I had ever been.

ELEVEN

Directions Home

My father's got to walk this lonesome valley;
He's got to walk it by his self.
There's nobody here can walk it for him;
He's got to walk it by his self.

— **A. P. CARTER**
"Lonesome Valley"
Recorded by
the Original Carter Family, 1935

Except for that brief break from his active addiction while we visited the Alaskan wilderness, Dad was an exceedingly sick man through most of 1983. He had become severely addicted to pain pills and was taking enormous doses of them. He hid stashes of drugs everywhere and was becoming increasingly volatile and unavailable.

To make matters worse, he injured his hand and also developed some digestive problems that required surgery. During the operation, Dad's surgeons removed some of his internal organs and also found that he had actually grown extra bone onto his sternum.

Following the surgery, he overdosed in his hospital room. He was already hallucinating because of the morphine the doctors prescribed, plus he was taking his own drugs on top of the ones the medical staff gave him. We were all scared for him . . . and scared *of* him at times too. The family knew that if something wasn't done soon, Dad would die.

After the overdose, Mom and I organized an immediate intervention. We called our family members to be there with us and to write letters to be read during the confrontation. My Uncle Tommy, dad's brother, was there to offer support. This was the first intervention I had ever been a part of, the first time I was ever to go head to head against the disease and try to save Dad's life. Mom was scared, and so was I. Mostly, I was afraid of being alone.

With all the arrangements made, the day of the intervention came. I held Mom's hand as we sat down in the hospital meeting room with the rest of the family members who had come. A nurse directed Dad into the room, and he nervously sat down between Mom and me. I felt his tension and anticipation on top of my own; my palms were sweating, and my leg was bouncing up and down uncontrollably. I loved this man dearly and could not stand the thought of hurting him. But I also had a great dread of losing him as my friend. He was the dearest one I had ever had.

Earlier that day I had voiced my worries to my mother: "But what if I tell him these things I feel, that I'm scared he's going to kill himself, that he has embarrassed me in front of my friends, all of it, and he says, 'That's too bad,' and goes on doing the same thing? . . . What if he leaves us?"

I didn't want to lose Dad. I loved him to the core of my very being.

"Your father is always going to love you, son," Mom reassured me. "This man we are dealing with right now is not the Daddy you have always known. Your real father is hidden away behind this lost person we are going to approach today. I pray that the real man inside will come out and do what he must do to change. If fact, I have faith he will."

Mom rubbed my head and gave me a hug. I was still of an age when that kind of affection from my mother did not humiliate me. On that day, her familiar touch was greatly calming to me.

Now sitting beside Dad in that sad meeting room in Nashville's Baptist Hospital, I felt those creeping tendrils of panic returning to my gut. Holding in my quivering hand the letter I had written to him, I turned to him and smiled, trying to save face.

The man who had agreed to help us with the intervention—I'll call him Larry—had spent a long time in active recovery from addiction. He sat across the room from Mom, Dad, and me, with the rest of the family seated around the circle between us. Larry eyed Dad with contemptuous regard. I didn't understand it then, but now I realize it wasn't my father Larry so angrily stared down as we began. It was the disease of addiction he was showing his contempt for. It was easy to see that Larry had done this before.

"Do you know why we're all here, John?" Larry asked. His tone was sort of passive, as though he really didn't care whether Dad answered.

"I believe so," Dad said.

I felt the blood drain from my face. Now my whole body was trembling.

"You have hurt your family too long. The time has come for a change," Larry said evenly. "Each person in this room has written a letter to you, John, and each is going to read their letter to you, one by one. You need to know what your use of drugs has done to your family."

I looked at my father anxiously. He seemed defeated, on the verge of tears. I had never seen him like that before. "I'll listen," was all he said.

We read our letters. Mom's letter told of her struggle year after year to deal with Dad's addiction and of how she could not go on fighting it anymore. She gave him an ultimatum: she loved him with all her heart, but if he did not get help and quit, she would leave him for good.

When my turn came, I read my letter slowly and cautiously. It was nearly impossible for me to tell Dad I was upset with him. I had only raised my voice to him once before, in that hotel room in Georgia. Reading a letter full of my grievances against him was not something I could easily do. I was afraid he would reject me, afraid I would make him angry with me.

Dad sat calmly through my reading, silent and motionless. Every time I glanced up from the paper, he was staring into my eyes. In my letter, I told him how tired I was of hearing his loud, labored breathing through the long nights on the road. I spoke about how awfully he had embarrassed me in front of my close friends by being totally stoned in their presence.

I cried a little, but not much. The real tears would come later.

Dad was meek. He asked for forgiveness and agreed to go to a treatment center. My father's true spirit was one of gentle love. God was present in the man.

I wanted to believe so badly that my beloved father would change forever.

A few days later, when he had fully recovered from the surgery, he canceled the rest of his tour, approved the arrangements for his stay at the Betty Ford Center, and left for California, where he would finally face his addictions, for the first time in a specialized recovery environment.

At the time, most treatment facilities for addiction and alcoholism offered twenty-eight-day programs that included a family week, when family members joined the recovering addict for all-day meetings, therapy sessions, and education about the twelve-step program and the disease of addiction.

Dad's disease had greatly sickened my mother and me, to the point where we needed recovery from its effects nearly as much as Dad did. So, on the third week of his stay there, Mom and I went to Palm Springs to meet Dad during family week—and, unknowingly, to meet our own sicknesses as well.

I walked into the center that first day feeling scared of what I would encounter there, fearful of the inevitable confrontations. What I found instead was the man I had feared lost. When I first saw Dad, he ran to me and picked me up. "My son! I'm so glad to see you!" he said joyously. The light was back in his eyes. He seemed brand new.

Then he turned to my mother. I felt their mutual apprehension. "You'll be glad you came this week, June," he said. "This is the best way of life for us. I now know who and what I am. We can be free through this program."

I was overjoyed and eager to forgive, but it wasn't so easy for Mom to believe. She had been hurt too deeply, wounded too many times. I sensed her hesitation as she regarded my father and absorbed his statement. She reached toward him and put her hands on either side of his face. "I love you, John," she said. "I can forgive, and I believe we *can* be free." Her resolve was clear, but her eyes were full of tears. She wanted so much to believe him.

Looking back, I think her heart was afraid to believe, possibly could *not* believe. But her love for this man was strong and unshakable. She held him close. She remembered her reaffirmed vows.

Mom and I spent the first three days at the Betty Ford Center in classes together, without Dad. We were being educated, for the first time, that addiction was a sickness of the body, mind, and spirit. Our newly gained knowledge helped us see that in some ways we were as ill as he was. We discovered that addiction is not a moral issue, and we learned that Dad was not necessarily weak or bad because of his broken promises and lies— they were an inherent part of his sickness. I learned then, for the first time, that I based my own feelings and my own sense of well-being on Dad's sicknesses or wellness. When he was clearheaded and clean, I felt secure and at ease. When he was high, I felt fearful and vulnerable.

These classes stressed that I could feel safe no matter what Dad's condition was. For me, that was a totally new way of thinking. Sadly, although this ideal registered in my mind and I accepted it as truth at the time, I did not actually develop this healthiness within my heart until nearly twenty years later.

During those years, there had been nothing I hated more than drugs and addiction. I saw Dad's addiction as the thing that tore our family apart. I could not have dreamed, back then, that one day I would turn into the same person my father was. I could not have dreamed I would become just as lost in addiction as he ever was . . . or that the power of addiction could even seize my mother, who had fought it so hard and so long.

Mostly what I felt in those days was sadness and fear. Ironically, it was these feelings, unresolved, that would develop into one of the greatest angers I have ever had.

I know my mother found much healing during that week. She learned a new way of living, including effective tools for dealing with the addicts in her life. She did great work with her counselor, not only on her relationship with Dad, but also on her relationship with Rosey, who was hurtful and capricious in her addiction. Mom saw that she had enabled Rosey for many years, giving her money when she was in trouble and bailing her out of jail when she was arrested for DUI.

The change was evident when Rosey called Mom during family week, and amazingly, Mom didn't return the call. It was one of her first steps in practicing the concept of "tough love." Her counselor had instructed her not to talk to Rosey while we were there, and I saw Mom accept that guidance and put her recovery into practice. I saw God work in her life.

Mom had always kept a journal, and during family week she learned that journaling could be an important part of recovery. So her journal-keeping intensified; she seemed to write constantly. Recently I read the words she wrote during that time and saw a great and admirable spirit of forgiveness and acceptance. "I can love John for the man he is inside," she wrote. "I can accept him whether he is stoned or not. What matters is that I keep my heart close to God. Jesus will keep me safe."

Mom was quite strong then, becoming once again the utmost, unmovable force in my life. I constantly turned to her for strength.

On our fourth day in the center, we were to begin the group sessions with Dad. Other patients and their families would be there also. We would all sit in a large circle with a counselor and go over our issues.

This was the hardest part of the week for me, the part I had dreaded most.

Mom and I were staying in a hotel in downtown Palm Springs, and in the evenings we would go out to dinner. We didn't discuss our days at the center much but instead focused mainly on the food. I was excessively overweight at the time and also depressed. Food was becoming my own drug of choice back then, though it was years before I comprehended it.

On the day we walked into the meeting room for our first group session with Dad and the others, I had just eaten a big breakfast. I became overwhelmingly nauseated, even before Dad joined us. When he came in, the queasiness gripped me. I ran out of the room and barely made it to the bathroom before I threw up. I was enormously afraid, but I cleaned up, regained my composure, and returned to the session, sitting next to Mom in the circle of chairs. The session commenced.

Most of the time I spent in that meeting room is a blur to me now. There is little I remember that I feel the need to share. I did see my mother forgive my father there; I'm sure of that. Mom had been working hard on her issues, both by herself and with her counselors, and she had been writing extensively. It was a relief to me to see the light come back to her eyes.

There was great wisdom to be gleaned from those two days of group sessions; however, my greatest takeaway from that whole experience was anger, largely directed at myself. The counselors had urged me to tell Dad how he had hurt me. They warned that I had held in so much anger for so long that I would explode if I didn't let it out.

It took some prodding, but finally, during one of the sessions, the rage and hurt came pouring out. "Dad, you hurt us all," I told him. "You don't know how I felt, seeing how you fell so deep for the pills. I lost you. I want you back again. *I want you back, Dad!*" This was a scene that would repeat itself later in our lives.

I ran out into the hall sobbing. I just couldn't take it anymore. I cried and cried and cried. There seemed to be no end to the pain; the tears just wouldn't stop. I ran into the bathroom and looked into the mirror, disgusted with myself.

"Never cry again!" I screamed at the reflection I saw. "Never! Never cry again!"

I repeated the words over and over, promising myself that I would never again shed a tear for my father. From that day forward, I vowed to be as unfeeling as stone, solid and cold. I would not feel *anything*. I would not let him hurt me again.

The family week sessions were healing for us in many ways. Mom improved considerably, Dad got clean and stayed that way for some time, and I gained greater understanding of how deadly addiction could be, not only to the addict, but to his or her family as well. But ironically, another part of me suffered severely from my experience at the treatment center; the consequences of that experience affected my life for years to follow. I kept my vow to stuff my feelings and hide my anger. I held my emotions prisoner, never letting them see the light of day, and as the counselors had predicted, my anger became my own private pain.

It wasn't long before I first experienced being drunk and set my feet upon the inevitable path toward addiction. It wasn't long before I became that which I so greatly despised.

TWELVE

New and Old Beginnings

Oh, Lord, God, have mercy on us all—
again. If you don't mind, Sir, please.

—JUNE CARTER CASH
From the Heart

I loved seeing the sparkle return to my mother's eyes during my early teen years. One day in the winter of 1983, Mom came to me, giggling, and said she and Dad were going on a second honeymoon. They just went to our home in Jamaica, but I'm sure it was a blessed trip.

At that point in their career, Dad wasn't at the top of the charts and was somewhat stifled creatively. But he could still sell two or three thousand seats at halls all around the Western Hemisphere, and Mom was always right there at his side. She would kick off her shoes and dance on stage, acting like a teenager. Their popularity might have slipped a little, but they were still considered a success story in the music industry, proving they could overcome difficulties and stand the test of time as husband and wife, as friends, and as entertainers.

In 1984 we went to Australia and spent quite some time in the outback with our family's close friends Dr. Con Potanin and his wife, Annie. On a

July tour, we were in the Australian winter, though the climate was still warm and moderate. Dad was usually the real adventurer while Mom liked to take Jeep rides through the bush to watch for Australia's amazing wildlife. That's not to say she wasn't afraid to step out a little herself.

One day, she and I set out to walk three miles down a trail through the bush to a designated meeting spot along a river. The trail dropped a thousand feet from the top of a large hill to the valley below. From the top of the hill, the walk appeared to be fairly easy, but once we were on the trail, we found it to be quite grueling. At one point the trail ahead seemed to disappear completely into some sort of rock maze.

"Mom, let's go back." I pleaded.

"Son, the good doctor suggested we follow this trail and said it would lead us to a cathartic river, and I believe him. Let's keep going. He says the waters there have great healing properties." She headed off without waiting for my reply.

I watched her disappear into the stand of rocks then quickly trotted after her, with thoughts of the many Australian poisonous snakes likely hiding under every other rock. It took me a minute to catch up with her. I tried to catch my breath while asking her, "What if the trail doesn't lead to the river, Mom? What if we get lost?"

She smiled back. "Just put one foot in front of the other, son. I promise we'll make it." It was evident she was sure of herself, much more than I.

We walked for what seemed like hours, but more than likely it was about thirty minutes, following the rocky path through stands of fragrant eucalyptus trees. I spent much of the time looking up, trying unsuccessfully to catch sight of a koala in the canopy above. Not watching where I was stepping, several times I lost my footing and tripped over rocks or branches in the trail.

We finally rounded one last turn in the path, and there was the river. I was exhausted and relieved. Mom smiled at me knowingly. We trekked upstream until we reached a spot where a road crossed the river, and there was Dad, standing in the dark water up to his knees, a fishing pole in hand.

"Son, I just caught a catfish! Funniest-looking catfish I've ever seen. Come join me!" he called.

Mom watched me go to him. I felt her smile on my back.

What comes to me as I think of this time is Mom's sense of certainty, her faith that things were unfolding as they should. She believed that God had a plan for us all and that if we listened to his quiet voice, we would hear his purpose for our lives. She told me many times that we are all children of God, that his hope is that we will rise to the occasion of this life and seize the day, living it to our fullest.

She believed that when we failed, God was quick to forgive. She pointed out to me often the words of Romans 3:23: "All have sinned and fall short of the glory of God," but reminded me that Jesus had died to pay the price for those sins. She cherished the Lord's Prayer, especially the part that asks God to "forgive us our trespasses as we forgive those who trespass against us." And she ended her book *Among My Klediments* with the prayer, "Help me, God, to live each day for You."[1]

Mom always tried to live that way, to the utmost, with her faith as her guide. If she judged others, she tried to base her judgment on their hearts and potential before their deeds and actions. She was the first to find the light in dark times, the first to look up and say, "Press on." This was the mother I knew in my early teens. She was the consummate traveler, the master entertainer, and, to many people, a spiritual guide. She was trustworthy and consistent; she held her standards high and was as honest as anyone I have ever known.

During that brief time, she was more than just a mother to me; she was a friend. We were two people who had suffered hard times together, and now we were clear of them. Not only that, but Dad was back. He was the same jovial, fun-loving friend who had been gone for so long.

Mom, Dad, and I spent a week in New York in the spring of 1984 while Dad recorded an album. Instead of sitting alone in the apartment, as I'd done in the past while we were in New York, I went sightseeing, shopping, to movies, and out to eat with Mom. We laughed and spent time together, just the two of us, simply having fun. Those days are some of my favorite memories of her. She and I were free then in our hearts.

But somehow, toward the end of that year, I began to slip away. It was then that I got drunk for the first time. I don't know how I could ever have thought that getting drunk was something I should do. After all, I'd had a thorough education in what addiction was and what pain it could cause. It should have been clear to me that I had great potential for becoming an addict myself.

Nevertheless, when the opportunity arose for me to drink with a friend, I took it. A buddy and I shared a dozen wine coolers then sat in the hot tub at our Hendersonville home for several hours one night while Mom and Dad were on the road and K was sound asleep. I became sick and threw up, but that didn't deter me. As soon as I had another chance to drink, I got drunk again. I was fourteen, and somehow I insulated myself from reality, thinking I would be different than my father and the other addicts in my family.

My slipping away from them occurred in many ways. Perhaps it was a natural progression that many teenagers follow, but however it happened, I was no longer the close friend to Mom and Dad I once had been. I never told them about my drinking or drug use, and even though they had to suspect it, at least later on, they never asked. The subject was simply never mentioned. Mom and I seldom talked like we once had talked; I was too busy, too caught up in my own agenda.

Mom and Dad lived their life primarily on the road. It wasn't easy, but they both loved it. Although I accompanied them regularly in the summers, during most of the school year, I stayed at home with K. When they did come home from touring, neither of them stayed very long before Dad set off for Bon Aqua and Mom headed to New York or to Virginia to visit her cousins there.

By the time I was fifteen, I was getting drunk most weekends, and I was further away from my mother emotionally than I had ever been.

Then, sometime in the mid-eighties, Dad began using drugs again. Mom tolerated his usage and kept her "eyes on the goal," as she often said. Dad had fallen back into his old pattern of getting better, getting clean, and then getting back to his old ways. I saw the up-and-down pattern continue for many years, with Mom tolerating and forgiving and, somehow, holding on to her strength.

As Dad fell deeper into that downward spiral, I likewise continued my own descent into the darkness. Meanwhile Mom kept her faith and constantly "lifted us up."

THIRTEEN

Back on the Gospel Road

There is going to be a meeting in the air
In that sweet, sweet by-and-by.
I am going to meet you, meet you over there
In that home beyond the sky.

The singing you will hear never heard by mortals' ears
Will be glorious, I do declare.
And God's own Son will be the leading one
At that meeting in the air.

— **A.P. CARTER**
"Meeting in the Air"
Recorded by
the Original Carter Family, 1940

Mom's faith in God was her driving force, her radiant light. She always focused on the good, the promise of better things in the life ahead. But the chief, defining characteristic of her remarkable Christian walk was that unfathomable ability to forgive those who hurt her the most, though some of us did it over and over.

Her faith had become the inspiration for a big step in Mom and Dad's career about the time I was born. For years they had dreamed of finding a way to tell the life of Christ in song, and finally that dream came true when they went into production on their film *Gospel Road*. Their love, though forged in struggle and music, had grown in strength because of their shared love for God.

Dad had rededicated his life to God, and he and Mom always prayed together. They had offered their talents to God to use in carrying out his plan, and they had faith that *Gospel Road* was a part of that plan. Dad wrote the script, but I know Mom was involved in every step of the production as an editor, a sounding board for Dad's ideas, and even as co-writer. It was her way to be there for the God she loved and the man she adored. She earnestly offered her inspiration and soul to the project.

So, in the early seventies, they had traveled to the Holy Land, and with the help of some dedicated professionals, made *Gospel Road* a reality. They considered it the most important work of their lives together. Still

Courtesy of John Carter Cash

The Gospel Road program cover from the Los Angeles premiere, 1974.

sold on DVD more than thirty years later, *Gospel Road* has touched people the world over.

I was just a toddler when Mom and Dad made their movie in the Holy Land. In 1992, I went back there with them; it was to be our final trip together to this land of bountiful inspiration that would forever mean so much to them.

We went to the Dead Sea and to Jericho, and then we traveled up the Jordan River to the Sea of Galilee. Dad was in considerable pain on this trip. His jaw had broken some two years before, due to some faulty dental work. The result was chronic nerve damage that would plague him the rest of his life. He was distracted, though very dedicated to the spiritual import of the trip. It was not long before that he had his jaw wired shut and he could only eat food chopped in a blender and sucked in through a straw. Mom was very thin during that trip, but otherwise in good health. She was bright in those days, full of energy and a joy to be around.

On the other hand, I was dealing with major depression. I had been to my first treatment center the year before for alcohol and drug addiction, and although the treatment center had helped, I frequently fell into moods when everything seemed hopeless. My parents tended to let me work through my own struggles and rarely offered help unless I asked. Up until then I'd been very private about my pain and kept it hidden inside. But when I had finally come to them for help, my parents had stood behind me.

I had always written music and poetry, but during that time I'd been in a miserable dry spell. By the time we arrived in Jerusalem, however, I was beginning to come out of that shell and feel some creativity reemerging.

Dad's and my addictions never stopped my mother from loving us and believing in us. It was the same for my sisters. Mom was loving and generous, thoughtful and caring, and she could always find a reason to look up, to believe that the best in a person would eventually come out. God surely gave her this wisdom for a reason. It was as if she could see through the veil of misery. Although the spirit of disease might torment her loved ones, sometimes making us hard and vicious, she saw beyond that ugliness into the heart of her child or husband, finding the beauty within us. That's what she continually focused on, the goodness in us rather than the darkness, and our time in the Holy Land was an example of that attitude.

One morning, in our Jerusalem hotel, I called Mom's room and told her I didn't want to go out that day. She had planned for us to go to the Dead Sea and then on to Qumran, an ancient archaeological site built in the time of Christ by the Essenes, the religious order to which John the Baptist belonged.

"I really don't feel like going, Mom," I told her. "I have some reading I'd like to do, and I love the view of the Mount of Olives from my window. Besides, I'm still jet-lagged."

My excuses must not have sounded all that convincing. "Can I come see you, son?" Mom asked.

"Oh, all right," I conceded. "Come on down, and we'll talk."

Mom came into the room, sat on the side of my bed, and smiled. I lay on the couch, still in my pajamas.

"I know right now life may seem to have you in the dumps," she said, "but son, this too shall pass."

"I'm just incredibly tired," I said, my heart low.

"I'm sure the things you'll see today will be remarkable and wonderful. Did your father ever tell you what Bob Dylan said when John told him we were returning here on this trip? He said the light here is different, and that things just *look* different because of it."

Dad *had* already told me what Bob had said, and I hadn't noticed any change in the light. But still, hearing Mom mention it again in her soft, familiar voice, I felt the slightest hint of intrigue.

She reached out and rubbed my head. By this time, that gesture embarrassed me to no end, but on that day I once again felt comforted. She gave me a look of tender understanding. "Pick up your mat and walk, John Carter," she said, repeating Jesus's words to the crippled man who lay beside the Pool of Bethesda. Mom always knew the right scripture to go with any particular moment; she had a remarkable way of pulling verses out of her hat, or rather, her memory, whenever they were most needed.

I sighed, accepting her request. "I'll get dressed," I said.

The ride down into the Dead Sea Valley was beautiful. At Qumran, I walked up the hill alone while my parents sat for a while on some chairs near the dig, watching the workers. It was a hot, windy day; the temperature was at least ninety degrees Fahrenheit. The desert hills surrounding us were pocketed with innumerable caves. It was in one of those caves that the Dead Sea scrolls had been found. The land is truly a place of mystery and splendor.

There are a few times in my life when I feel God was directly showing me something or teaching me a lesson. That day I witnessed one of the most unusual and inexplicable things I have ever seen. As I reached a rise about half a mile from the parking area, something black caught my eye. I looked up and saw a large raven hovering no more than fifteen feet above me. The raven was behaving in an unusual manner, but the stranger thing was that in its beak it held a black glove.

I stared up at the bird, trying to absorb what I was seeing. It continued to hover there in the sky with the glove in its beak for at least thirty seconds. Finally, it gave out a loud squawk and dropped the glove a few feet away from me. The wind whipped the glove away, and I excitedly raced after it, following as it tumbled near a stony ledge. I watched where the glove landed and carefully scrambled over through the dust and rocks to reach it. I don't know what I expected, really, but when I picked it up, the glove was quite plain, made out of some sort of dark, felt-like material.

I carried it back down to my parents and related the story to them. My mother looked at me with that wonderful sparkle in her eye; she didn't seem surprised in the least by what I'd told her. "I think God is trying to say he has his hand on you, son."

I remember thinking at the time that I certainly didn't come anywhere close to feeling God's hand on me. But what Mom said that day has stayed with me ever since. And though I may have doubted it at the time, I know now that Mom was telling me what she knew to be true: that God was watching over me and knew I would come out the far side of that depression stronger and wiser. Mom never failed to believe that God would keep her loved ones safe. It took quite awhile for me to get to that same place spiritually.

I lost that glove before we came back to America. I think of it sometimes and shake my head. What did it mean, if anything at all? Was it all just a strange coincidence? But Mom always taught me to believe in miracles, to see that they are in fact commonplace. So I can't help but feel certain that such an unusual incident happening at such a powerful spot must surely have had some sort of meaning.

Mom said that day if I really opened my eyes, I would walk around in total amazement, and that's exactly what happened. From there, we went to the Dead Sea, where I bathed in the heavy, salty, mineral-filled water. I floated in the sun. I cried, and I prayed. My soul healed.

I pray my words do justice to describing the strongest core of Mom's being, a part of her I remember most brilliantly: June Carter Cash loved as deeply as anyone I have ever known, and she was the most forgiving person I have ever known.

Mom gave all she had to her family in spirit, soul, and body. Sometimes, when the night is dark and I question my path, I think of the simple wisdoms she gave me, and suddenly the way seems straighter and the morning seems closer:

God has a plan for you.

This too shall pass.

Press on.

FOURTEEN

The Fall of Camelot

Well, the world keeps spinnin' around
And I'm almost outta sight.
I keep slippin into hell,
I can't seem to get it right.

—JUNE CARTER CASH
"Wings of Angels"
Recorded by June in 1998

Mom loved movies. She would sit up late at night and watch films, old and new, of various kinds. She was always charmed by the fine costumes and jewelry included in the period films of the Victorian age. She read quickly and frequently, always absorbing and digesting information. She was always running her mental gears, incessantly moving her lips, whether speaking or not. It was just another part of her charm.

She liked to call the Hendersonville lake house Camelot, and she thought of it as her and Dad's private kingdom. She referred to the women who worked at the house as her ladies-in-waiting. There were many of them through the years, but a select few came and stayed. These employees learned early on that they could be asked to do anything and everything for the family: clean the toilets, plant the flowers, greet the guests, pick up the kids at school, or go get one of the girls out of jail at three o'clock in the morning. Anything at all. From the beginning, they needed to understand this was the nature of the job.

Anna Bisceglia was one of these ladies-in-waiting who came and stayed. She had come to America from Italy in the 1960s, and her husband, Armando, was the brother-in-law of the man who had built the Hendersonville house. Armando worked for my parents, too, as their head of security for many years. Anna was the housemaid, and she was always present, ready to lend Mom a hand and serve her in any way she felt needed.

One of the longest-lasting employees was Peggy Knight, who began working for the family in the early 1970s when she was quite young. She was initially hired to care for Grandma Maybelle after Grandpa Ezra passed away. Peggy was a wonderful cook.

Camelot's large staff, comfortable and spacious accommodations, and beautiful outward appearance made it a pleasant place to live, but that didn't keep its occupants from enduring heartache and crises. Given all the problems Mom had lived through due to the devastating addictions of her husband and children, it seems almost impossible to believe that she would ever fall under the spell of drugs herself. But she did.

I first remember seeing and fearing Mom's addiction in 1993 when we were performing a series of shows in Branson, Missouri. Mom and Dad lived in a house on the Arkansas border and drove to Branson every day to perform in a theater there. I was living that summer in a small apartment in Branson. Before one of those performances, I came into Mom's dressing room unannounced and found her laid out on the floor, already dressed in her stage outfit. I rushed to her side, and as my heart started that familiar terrified pounding, I felt an awful sense of déjà vu.

"Mom! Wake up! Please, Mom!"

If it weren't so tragic, her response would seem almost comical, like something inspired by one of her old Carter Sisters routines. She rolled over, her long hair splayed over her face, opened her eyes, and focused on me deliberately. "I am awake," she answered calmly. "I was in meditation."

Puzzled but not yet willing to believe the unthinkable, I left the room, and Mom went on to perform the show. Although she was slightly giddy and most definitely under the influence of something, she performed well.

It wasn't long until my puzzlement became serious concern. And I wasn't the only one who was worrying about June Carter Cash.

When I was young, my mother was as sharp as a tack; she was always on top of things. She had a great memory, could instantly strike up a conversation with anyone about anything, loved to laugh, and stood out as the brightest, most charming woman in any room full of people. I said earlier that while I was young, my parents were everything to me. When Dad slipped away from me into his addictions, my heart was broken, and I felt cheated, angry at the drugs that had stolen him from me. But then Mom was still there, still constant, still the strong one.

In her later life, that bright and reliable woman also went away.

For so long Mom had obsessed over the addictions of her husband, her daughters, and her son. Next she moved into denial. Then came the time, I believe, when she had simply had enough, when the struggle with the addicts in her life overcame her strength and resolve. With no better way of describing it, I think the cumulative mental, physical, and emotional pain combined in such a way that the drug use eventually seemed okay to her.

She would never have acknowledged that she too was an addict. I believe she always felt the illusion of control, as though the drugs were her friends, her helpers. I think she thought of herself as the master, not the slave, of the pills she took. After all, she never got angry, fell down, or picked a fight with her loved ones when she was under the influence of narcotics. She simply stopped speaking in full sentences and went off into her own world. Her mind was not the same.

Perhaps you could blame her drug use on those early days when she had traveled with Mother Maybelle and her sisters and everyone had a big bag of medicines, over-the-counter stuff. Whatever the problem was, you took a pill, and the problem went away.

Later in life, Mom had chronic pain in her legs that tormented her and sometimes kept her awake all night long. She also had suffered a back injury earlier in life, and although it had healed and the doctors insisted there was no reason for any more pain, the pain persisted. It seemed natural, I'm sure, to pop a pill to take away the hurt or to help her sleep, just as she had done all her life. The difference was that in her early years the pain had occurred occasionally and the pill was probably an aspirin. Now, the pain was perpetual—either physical pain in her body or emotional pain in her heart—and the pills were prescription narcotics.

She could still pop a pill and find peace. But, in doing so, she found her way into addiction.

Camelot was crumbling. To outsiders, the House of Cash probably seemed like the same successful, thriving enterprise it had always been. But behind the public curtain, drugs were in control. And not only of my parents' lives, but mine also.

In 1992, I went through my second full-term treatment at a center for drug and alcohol addiction. Earlier that year I had reached another bottom. I lived in San Bernardino, California, for six months, near the treatment center, working my recovery program.

The following summer was when I found Mom "in meditation" on the floor of her dressing room in Branson. And as the weeks passed after that, I saw her grow increasingly sick and confused. My parents' employee Kti Jensen and I set up an intervention for my mother. By this point, I knew exactly how these things worked. Kti and I sat down with her in her dressing room and laid out our feelings and concerns for her.

Dad, who had just spent a month at the same California treatment center as I, was clean and positive then; however, he would not be a part of our intervention. Mom and I had often shared our misery about Dad's addictions, but I could never talk to Dad about Mom's drug use. He lived with his own denial, and he would not challenge her.

I know he loved my mom more than anything in the world; he cherished her and she him. They were business partners and lovers, helpmeets and encouragers. In the past, when one was weak, the other had been strong. But sadly, as the years passed, they became each other's alibi for addiction. I know my father felt he had no place in confronting her about her own addiction after he had put her through hell about his. He felt he had no right.

So that day Kti and I began what we hoped would be an intervention that would change the track Mom was on. We had arranged for her to go to a treatment center, as so many others in her family had done. But our plan had no effect at all. Mom refused to hear what we had to say. She always had an amazingly powerful will, and she used it that day.

"I am just fine, John Carter!" she said. "I am in total control of myself, and you had best let well enough alone!"

"Mom, I only love and care for you. Please listen! This thing is bigger than you." I knew the words to say because this same logic had already been used on me several times by this point in my life. Now I tried it on her, but it was no use. She was like a rock. She ran Kti and me out of her dressing room.

Afterward, Mom straightened up for a while, probably to prove to us that she *could* do it on her own. She *could* master the drugs. But that arrangement didn't last long.

I never again tried to push Mom into a treatment center. She was in control, and that was that. I simply learned, in time, to let her have her own sicknesses. The truth is, she wasn't always under the influence of drugs in the later years of her life, but there was quite a bit of time when she was.

Due to her heavy drug use, her mind wasn't what it once was. It wasn't easy, but I learned to know and accept a different woman as my mother in the last decade of her life. I never stopped loving Mom or believing in her, but there were times when I was frustrated by her behavior and her emotional abandonment.

Of course, I'm sure the people around me were equally frustrated with my behavior. After all, I was usually high, too. But just as certainly as I denied my addiction, Mom denied hers as well.

The Virginia house was her place of peace, and after her sisters Helen and Anita died, going there was the closest thing she could do to get back to her roots. Her cousin and lifelong friend Fern Salyer was still there, as she is now, and they visited often. When Mom was back in the mountains, she was a little country girl again. She would go to the antique stores in Gate City and Kingsport every week, and when the shop owners saw her coming, they knew there would be a good sale.

The Virginia house was full of clutter, "klediments" as Mom called them, using the old mountain word for treasures. Every chair and couch was draped with lace and covered with pillows; every nook and cranny was filled with a piece of furniture. The porch was filled, too, and all the outbuildings were packed full.

My father, in contrast, always liked simple things and preferred an uncluttered decorating style. However, he tolerated Mom's tastes and eccentricities gracefully. I found photos of the lake house from late in 1967, before Dad and Mom married. They show wide-open rooms with very little furniture and only a few scattered mementos. I have a few of those items still: a bust of an Indian's head, gilded bookends, a drawing of Abraham Lincoln. These things remind me of how my father changed to bring my mother into his life.

Dad never showed his concerns for Mom's addictions in the same way she had shown her concern for his. He gave her space and distance, yet I saw him love her more and more as each year passed. When Dad's eyesight failed and he could no longer read, he spent hours at a time sitting with Mom, just watching television or listening to her talk. They would nap often, and they took their medicine together. They were each other's partner and soul-tender.

Although they enabled each other's addiction and sicknesses, there was an undeniable beauty to the love they shared later in life. They had learned the art of unconditional forgiveness, and each accepted the other totally. They were still the most beautiful couple I have ever seen.

The king and queen of Camelot had suffered greatly and for a long time. By the late 1990s, the beauty of their youth was slipping away. And although my father's career gained momentum in this period, physically, he was going downhill. When he stopped performing in 1997 due to his failing health, Mom retired from the road with him, joining him in semi-retirement as she had joined him in his career.

But they didn't stop working. Dad continued recording for Rick Rubin and American Recordings. And even though he spent countless hours in the hospital due to diabetes and a mysterious neurological disorder, he spent just as much time in the studio.

Maybe some people expected Mom to disappear from the music scene once her husband and on-stage partner had stepped out of the brightest spotlights, but that's not what happened. Despite the narcotics' effect on her mind, and despite physical ailments and challenges, she had always kept up with Johnny Cash creatively and productively, and she wasn't about to stop now.

She would soon be going into the studio herself.

FIFTEEN

Bear Me Up on Wings of Angels

His love shall control me through life and in death,
Completely I'll trust to the end.
I'll praise Him each hour of my last fleeting breath,
Shall sing of my soul's Best Friend.

— A.P. CARTER
"Anchored in Love"
Recorded by
the Original Carter Family, 1927

The most valuable "klediment" to my mother was her family: not just the seven children she claimed but also her parents, sisters, in-laws, cousins, aunts, uncles, and grandchildren. She taught me to love them all too. I grew up with all of my grandparents nearby. While Grandpa Ezra and Grandma Maybelle lived a few miles away in Madison, my Cash grandparents lived across the street from our Hendersonville home for most of my life.

I stayed a few times with Grandma Maybelle as a baby when, for whatever reason, Mom and Dad couldn't take me along and Grandma Maybelle wasn't traveling with them either. I was only four when Grandpa Ezra died in 1974, and I don't remember much about that time except my mother's sad face. I do know she kept working, though, and Grandma Maybelle went back on the road with her for a period of time. When Grandma Maybelle passed in 1978, my mother, and the world with her, wept.

I remember these losses only through the eyes of a child and then as a teenager, but each loss was harder to handle. Dad's father, my Grandpa Ray, died in 1986. By the time my Grandma Carrie Cash died in 1991, I was in the throes of addiction and was simply incapable of dealing with it. I loved her dearly, as I had loved all my grandparents, but I avoided pain associated with death at all cost. The day she died, I developed a very real pain in my stomach. I went to the hospital for tests, but they all gave inconclusive results. I remember lying in that hospital bed on the day of her funeral, nearly incapacitated by pain pills while regretting that I wasn't there to support my parents.

They grieved over the deaths but went on with their lives and continued to work. They both had been raised to keep on going even when times were hard and hearts were broken. It was their legacy. Another part of Mom's legacy, in addition to her family's music and its strong work ethic, was her unshakable faith. She learned the gospel and the Bible mainly from her father. Grandpa Ezra was an exceptionally well-read man with a great love for spiritual writings. I remember once when I was a boy visiting my parents' friends and being awed by their huge library.

"Look at all the books, Mom!" I said. "Do you think they read them all?"

Mom looked at me and smiled. "No, son. The only person I ever knew who read every book he ever bought was your Grandfather Ezra."

Ezra had thousands of books, and according to Mom, he read them all.

My mother shared her father's love for knowledge and reading. She read faster than anyone I have ever known. I remember her reading the very long novel *The Thornbirds* in only one night. The extraordinary thing was that she actually retained what she read. She was bright, intellectual, and quick witted.

While Mom was close to both her parents, she especially treasured

Maybelle and considered her to be the perfect mother and greatest musician in the world. It may seem strange to fans of her music now, but although Maybelle was considered the "Belle of Appalachia," she had no idea, herself, of the great influence she had on the world and music in general. Likewise, Grandma Maybelle held no real mythical importance to me when I was a child.

I remember going over to her house in Madison, Tennessee, and playing in the yard. To me, she was just the tender, loving grandmother who made the great pickles. Amazingly, I kept that nonchalant attitude about Grandma Maybelle until the late 1990s, when Mom needed a musician—ideally, a girl who could play several instruments and also sing—to help her with some shows connected with her new album, *Press On*.

Dad's longtime friend and engineer David Ferguson—everyone called him Ferg—suggested that Mom audition Laura Weber, a young woman he'd worked with on the bluegrass circuit who had a great voice and who played fiddle, guitar, and mandolin. Like many Nashville professionals, Laura worked as a waitress to supplement her unstable musician's wages.

Mom invited her out to the lake house for the audition, and she, Dad, and Laura sat around picking and talking for an hour or so, then Mom said, "Thank you, honey. We'll give you a call."

Mom called her back the next day and asked her to help with a few gigs, including a big *Press On* party she was planning at the lake house. I was on a fishing trip to Florida when Mom hired Laura, but I began to work with her a couple of weeks later when Mom asked us to put together a band to play for the party. I had met Laura once before while playing music, but somehow nothing had clicked back then. The band we formed for Mom's *Press On* party and the related performances was called The Living Circle and included Laura on the fiddle and me singing back-up and playing guitar.

During the month of rehearsals leading up to the party, we got

**Laura Cash and June Carter Cash perform
at her *Press On* party, May 15, 1999.**

acquainted. I was going through a painful divorce and wasn't looking to
get involved again anytime soon. But I was fascinated by Laura. To be honest, she was one of the first really independent women I'd ever gotten to
know. She was probably a lot like my mother had been while she was
working and coping with the pressures of being a single mom.

Laura wasn't a mom yet, but she was working hard and surviving
totally on her own, juggling her waitress and music jobs. She also had a
great closeness and deep relationship with her own family, who lived in
Oregon. She owned an old house that she had restored herself, and she
had been involved in the music business for twelve years, especially in the
bluegrass end of it. I was impressed.

During rehearsals, Laura, who seemed to have a thorough knowledge
not only of bluegrass but of traditional Appalachian country music, might
call out a Carter Family number for us to do, and, as strange as it may
seem, I was usually the only one who wasn't familiar with it. Laura, on the

other hand, was a huge fan of the Carter Family and seemed to know their music inside and out. She would make it her goal to teach me a true love for the music of my own family.

One day during a break she said to me, "What's the deal? You're Mama Maybelle's grandson, and you don't know her music? You're what—twenty-eight? Twenty-nine? Isn't it about time you learned this stuff?"

I remember looking at her and thinking that sure, I'd sung Carter Family music all my life, but I'd never really looked into the wealth of music in the catalog. After all, what young kid listens to his *grandparents'* music? Yes, I knew my roots went deep in Appalachian music, and that was cool, but I was into the more modern sounds.

Yet there sat a beautiful, blonde-haired, talented *young* woman who lived and breathed for the music of the mountains, *my grandmother's music.* I became fascinated with the Carter Family catalog . . .

One day Laura handed me a paper bag with a big "12" written on it in black marker. It was her Carter Family CD collection, and she wanted every one of those CDs back. "I work hard for little money," she said earnestly. "I can't afford to buy new ones, so don't lose any of them."

I took the CDs home and listened to them over and over again, gaining a whole new appreciation for the legacy I was a part of. That's how I fell in love with my grandmother's music . . . and also with Laura Weber.

Sixteen

Drawing Pictures in the Sand

I'll be waiting on the far side banks of Jordan.
I'll be sitting drawing pictures in the sand.
And when I see you coming, I will rise up with a shout,
And come running through the shallow water reaching for your hand.

— TERRY SMITH
"Far Side Banks of Jordan"
Recorded by Johnny Cash and
June Carter Cash, 1998

Mom had come to me in 1998, excited and energetic, asking me to co-produce a project for her. She wanted to name the album *Press On* after one of her favorite phrases from A.P. Carter's song "Diamonds in the Rough." I was happy to be a part of the project.

But she wanted to record at our log cabin, a rugged little structure tucked into the woods on the hill above the lake house. Dad had the cabin built as a hideaway where he could read and rest in solitude. It was a pleasant and comfortable place, but it wasn't a studio. There wasn't enough gear and equipment there to record more than one or two musicians at once. My father had recorded some music there before, around 1994, that in fact had made it to his first *American Recordings* CD with Rick Rubin, but not much since then.

Still, if that's what Mom wanted, we decided to just bring in the necessary equipment and make it happen. Those sessions would be the beginning of the cabin's transformation into an authentic recording studio.

Mom had signed with Small Hairy Dog Records, a Los Angeles–based label. She was comfortable with the owner, Vicki Hamilton, who had started in the music business working with rock bands in the 1980s. I was to co-produce the CD with the engineer, Hollywood native J. J. Blair.

Vicki and J.J. showed up in Nashville with two massive cases of recording equipment, and we hauled it to Hendersonville and moved it into the one-room cabin. By the next day, the small cabin bulged with miles of cords and cables, mic and music stands, soundboards, guitars, drums, a mandolin, bass, keyboard, and guitars, and all the people necessary to play them or make them work. In addition to Vicki and J.J., Mom and me, the room also held, at various times, Dad, Norman Blake, Hazel Johnson, Marty Stuart, Dave Roe, Rick Lonow, Jason Carter, and my sister Rosey. It was quite a houseful, but finally we were set up and ready to go. We went over song ideas together and picked our favorites from Mom's original songs and also the Carter Family standards.

Working in the studio with Mom was usually quite relaxed as we normally saw the music eye to eye, and that was the case this time too. There was always an overall element of spontaneity in the studio, especially when Mom was involved. You never knew exactly what was going to happen or how the sound would actually come together.

She was consistently creative during that project. She wanted the recording to have quite a bit of spoken dialogue—and she gave us plenty! She always had a few words or a story to go along with each song. Sometimes she would give an introduction; other times she would tag on a tidbit of dialogue after the music had stopped. Sometimes she was simply talking to the guys in the band who, as usual, she called her babies, feeling maternal because she had helped some of them get their start in the music business.

June posing backstage with her family after performing at a Johnny Cash show (from left: June, Anita, Ezra, Maybelle, and Helen).

June plays with baby Carlene outside her parents' home in Madison, Tenn., in 1956.

Onstage with Johnny Cash.

Among other things, June
Carter was known for her
beautiful long brown hair.

June sits on the front porch with her two
daughters, Carlene and Rosey, c. 1963.

June poses on a motorcycle outside her parents' home in 1956.

Johnny and June performed a show in Sioux Falls, S.D., March 12, 1968, eleven days after they were married.

June Carter Cash and Johnny Cash were known for their deep, enduring love.

Johnny and June in their last portrait together.

Courtesy of John Carter Cash

June Carter Cash, Carlene Carter, Rosey Nix, and Rosanne Cash.

Courtesy of John Carter Cash

June and Johnny Cash with Fern Salyer in Va.

Courtesy of John Carter Cash

Maybelle and Ezra Carter.

© Alan Messer www.alanmesser.com

June with Robert Duvall.

© Alan Messer www.alanmesser.com

Cousin Joe Carter and June in Maces Springs, Va.

© Alan Messer www.alanmesser.com

June Carter Cash and Willie Nelson.

Courtesy of John Carter Cash

June and her mother-in-law, Carrie Cash, at the House of Cash in 1986.

and Family

June, Bob Dylan, Carlene Carter, and Johnny Cash backstage at a Dylan concert.

John Carter, Laura, and their children; Joseph, Annabelle, and Jack.

Johnny, John Carter, Jessi Colter, Waylon Jennings, and June backstage at the Opry.

Johnny and June with Roy Clark on the set of *Hee Haw*.

June's family serenades her during grandchildren's week.

Billy Graham, June, Ruth Graham, and Johnny enjoy a day by the pool at their house in Jamaica.

Johnny and June with dear friend Jane Seymour.

The note in June's handwriting on the back of this photo says "fun stop on tour."

A playful moment between mother and son.

In Melbourne, Australia, March 1973.

June and John Carter at his high school graduation.

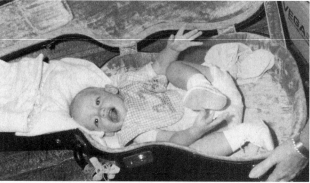

Life on the road means diaper changes in guitar cases for John Carter, 1971.

The young Cash family was constantly on the road,
very familiar with airports and hotels.

Annie Liebovitz preps Johnny
and June for a photo.

June and Johnny sing alongside the
Grahams at a Billy Graham Crusade
in Tampa, Fla., March 1979.

Despite her days spent traveling the world, June Carter Cash would always be a country girl at heart, with the hills of Virginia calling her home.

Sometimes what she says on *Press On* makes sense, and sometimes it's just for fun. For example, before the song "Tall Lover Man," she says,

[laughing] I'm tellin' you, I'm gonna give all of you guys—all of you—now, Dave, you've got to really shine this time, and Marty. Because this is the murder, babies. Well, it's just, we're all gonna jump in on this thing, and Rodney's playin' thumbs, and I'm playin' foot [laughs]. So we'll see what happens. This is [laughs] this one's really got—wait a minute, Norman, we've not even started! And it takes so long for this man to die in here. We'll just all start together at once, and then we'll kill that dude in just a little while.

Mom was the director, the bandleader, the vocalist, and the cheerleader. The band had to follow her, and it wasn't always easy because she seldom performed a song the same way twice. Thus, rehearsals weren't all that helpful, and chord charts, normally a necessity for the Nashville studio elite, were useless. It took a friend like musical virtuoso Norman Blake to hang in there with her, which he did masterfully.

There was no separation of the studio's sound tracks then. The upright bass and drums were on Mom's microphone, her autoharp and voice on the other microphones. The mics were picking up all the sound in the small room. Separation is typically quite important in recording, but listening back now, I see that what was lacking in sonic perfection is easily overlooked: these recordings are magic. However, the recording sessions were nothing short of a chaotic conglomeration, and it was only a miracle, or at least divine guidance, that made the project possible.

Despite the less-than-perfect technical arrangement and the casual atmosphere, we pressed on. Mom employed her magical way of turning her inabilities and shortcomings into endearing qualities. I had seen her do it many times on the stage and in the studio. Whenever she had lacked vocal ability, she had compensated with soul. Whenever she had felt that she appeared ungraceful, she had kicked off her shoes and danced even harder.

Her traditional personality shined through as the work for *Press On* continued. She was charming and strong, unique and beautiful, sometimes rolling into a word in the lyrics with the characteristic June Carter "growl." I remember her being quite bright and mentally present during the sessions for *Press On*.

This was a golden time for her. Where for years she had played the supporting role for my father, now Dad sat at her side, playing guitar and adding backup vocals. However, it was Dad who told the story of one of the most memorable songs on the album. He said,

June was in Jamaica, and I was delayed a few days getting there. This was back in '74, and she'd been sick. I was sick—tired, exhausted like we usually are when we get to Jamaica. I think we plan it on purpose so we'll have to stay in bed. [Mom laughs and says, "It's a good way to get there!"] Anyway, I had this song that I'd brought from Nashville. Well, I hadn't come from Nashville, I'd come from California. But I brought the song from Nashville. I think it was written by a schoolteacher. [Mom: "Terry Smith."] Terry Smith. Okay. Anyway I told June, "I've got something that'll make us both feel better." So there in the *drawring* room—up in New York they call it the *drawring* room—we sat down, and I sang her this song. And we both cried. And then we felt better.

Then they sang "Far Side Banks of Jordan" as a duet. They sat close, in front of the massive rock fireplace in the cabin, and looked into each other's eyes as they sang. Dad started off, his voice deep and solid:

I believe my steps are growing wearier each day,

Got another journey on my mind.

Lures of this old world have ceased to make me want to stay,

And my one regret is leaving you behind.

Then Mom sang these lines:

But if it proves to be His will that I am first to cross,

And somehow I've a feeling it will be,

When it comes your time to travel, likewise don't feel lost.

For I will be the first one that you'll see.[1]

In my memory I see them still, seated together, their heads almost touching, their eyes smiling at each other and their voices blending again just as they had so many times before. Looking back now, the moment holds enlightening significance to me. It was the final time I saw them both strong together.

After that, an alternating pattern of strength and sickness would emerge. In the coming years, if Dad was in the hospital or overpowered by addiction, Mom was the strong one, the spouse who managed to stay more in control, the who was clearer headed, capable of managing herself and the household. When Mom became sick, Dad would take on the strong-person role. One was always there to support the other, but after *Press On*, I never saw them strong at the same time again.

I had heard them sing "Far Side Banks of Jordan" many times, but to this day, their *Press On* recording of the song moves me in a way nothing else does. By that time, Dad had been sick for many years, and everyone in the room—and everyone in the family, including Dad himself—would have predicted that he would be the first to go.

But when they divided up the lyrics, it was Mom who sang the lines, "But if it proves to be His will that I am first to cross, and somehow I've a feeling it will be. . . ."

The thing that haunts me is the sadness and conviction I hear in her voice as she sings the words.

I can't help but wonder if somehow she knew . . .

SEVENTEEN

First Time to Headline

*Our lives are entwined with the people over the footlights;
we are a part of them.*

— JUNE CARTER CASH
Among My Klediments

When Mom went back on the road in support of her album *Press On*, it was the first time in her long career she had ever headlined. She played several engagements, including the *Late Show with David Letterman* and the Bottom Line, a well-known club in New York City. Dad went on the road with her, and for the first time, was there to back her up rather than to take center stage himself.

The band would start the show with a rousing instrumental version of "Back Up and Push," featuring Laura's characteristic fiddling, then Mom would take the stage and play most of the songs on her CD before she introduced Dad as her "very special guest." Then Dad would come out on stage and join her in performing "Far Side Banks of Jordan," "Jackson," and "If I Were a Carpenter." They would usually end the show together with "Will the Circle Be Unbroken?" and "Daddy Sang Bass."

We all knew Mom deserved the headliner's spotlight. She had spent too many years as a backup artist for whoever got top billing (mostly Dad), and now she was drawing the crowds on her own. Dad was glad not to have the headline spot and was there solely to support Mom. I was there, too, as a member of her backup band, The Living Circle. We played some fifteen dates through the summer of 1999; the crowds were good, and we had a lot of fun.

In the midst of going through the miserable process of getting a divorce that year, I enjoyed working with Laura, the vivacious young fiddle player. Laura and I were "just friends" at first. She was a fun and talented person to be with, and I was drawn to her spark and fire. I've often marveled since then how sometimes the love of your life just somehow comes along. When that happens, you have to grab hold and never look back. That's what I did.

During the *Press On* performances, Mom saw what was happening and happily played the matchmaker, creating reasons for Laura and me to be alone. "John Carter, why don't you go pick up Laura for rehearsal," she might say. "And stop by the music store to get me some autoharp strings. I need an extra set."

Not that I needed a lot of prompting. I had my own ideas for how I might spark a conversation or plan a way to be together. Laura laughs now at one of my more romantic but also comical gestures. When she wasn't working with Mom, she was still waiting tables to pay her bills. One night after she had worked late, I wanted to leave a little gift on her doorstep, so I got up at the crack of dawn and cut a large bouquet from Mom's rose garden. The part that still makes Laura laugh was that before leaving them on her porch, I stuck the roses in a brown paper sack and wrote on the outside, "Open outside—bugs."

Given the matchmaker role Mom was playing (or at least thought she was playing), it seems funny now to remember the morning in Jamaica the next year when I told my parents that Laura and I were getting married. She had come with us to Cinnamon Hill, and I planned to tell Mom and

Dad about my intentions at breakfast on our first morning there. So as we gathered around the breakfast table, just the four of us, I said, "Well, we're gonna get married in Oregon this summer, and we want y'all to be there."

"Oh, so soon!" Mom exclaimed, as if she'd just met Laura a minute ago.

Dad was quiet for a moment then answered, "Good. We'll be there, son. We'll be there."

And they *were* there when we were married on a beautiful farm near Laura's parents' home in Oregon in 2000. Mom beamed from the front row, and Dad, with one hand resting on the shoulder of my rambunctious son, Joseph, to keep him still, read 1 Corinthians 13, the "love chapter," as part of the wedding ceremony. One of our favorite photographs from the wedding is Dad leaning in to give Laura a kiss. Laura says he then whispered into her ear, "Now get pregnant!"

And she did just that. When our first child, a daughter, was born the next year, we named her Anna Maybelle. Laura also has been a loving stepmom

Photo by Tony Overman. Copyright © John Carter Cash

Johnny Cash kisses his daughter-in-law, Laura, at her wedding to John Carter on July 1, 2000.

to Joseph, my son from my first marriage. She's always been there for him for as long as he can remember, and they cherish each other dearly.

Our first year of marriage was hard, as I was drinking heavily. I struggled with addiction during these times: sober for a period, then I would go on a binge. I was unpredictable and more alone than would be expected for one who had such a wonderful family. It would still be a couple of years before I had finally had enough, before I allowed God to change my heart.

As my family expanded, I followed my mom's lead in realizing these loved ones—past and present—are my most important klediment. Like Mom, I treasure these dear ones beyond measure . . . and yet, by the choices Mom and I made, we caused our loved ones tremendous hurt.

My marriage to Laura has been the best thing that ever happened to me, but the wedding wasn't even on the horizon yet when Dad, Laura, and I joined Mom for her *Press On* performances. Mom's granddaughter (and my niece) Tiffany Lowe (Carlene's daughter), performed with us too, and, when she would come, my sister Rosey also played in the backup band.

Rosey was hard to predict during that time. She had begun using methamphetamine by then, and she had gone from being overweight and jovial to slim and dark humored. She was still prone to angry outbursts, and although her personality seemed to be ever changing, there was one thing that was always the same: you could count on Rosey to make a mess of things.

Although we had been close in our younger years, by then I was spending less and less time with Rosey, and when I did see her alone, it was on the few occasions when I used meth and cocaine myself. I was still drinking heavily, but speed wasn't my thing. And it certainly wasn't Laura's. There were times, however, when I did get the urge for speed or cocaine, and if I did, I knew where to go: to Rosey.

It may seem I hold her sickness against Rosey, that I am bitter now, but I'm not. I remember the kind and gentle person she was during my younger years. The Rosey she became in her later years simply was not the same person. I have since let her go to be with God. I love her still and remember the good times. I must always remember that those disgusting things I saw in Rosey were only reflections of myself back then. At times, Rosey and I were partners in our sickness, our drug usage, and our basic behavior. I firmly believe that if I were to progress with active addiction, I would wind up as she did.

Meanwhile, Mom continued to look upon her children as perfect, and she saw past our insanities as she sometimes grappled with her own problems. Some days during that time, Mom was still clearheaded and straight; other days she was distant and blank-minded. But whatever her condition in private, she was in her element when she stepped into the spotlight, singing for her fans and giving it her all.

The day in late 1999 when the Grammy Award nominees for 2000 were announced was a special day. I was with Mom and Dad at the lake house when the nominees were named, and we were overjoyed that Mom was up for best traditional folk recording.

I have to admit that I was also excited as co-producer of the CD. But mostly, I was excited for Mom. She had come so far in so many ways— from the little girl who had to compensate for having an off-key singing voice to become a Grammy-nominated artist, on her own this time (her previous Grammy wins were as a duet partner with Dad).

She had worked long and hard for this recognition, and while she still might not technically be the greatest singer, she had tremendous character and charisma. She was never afraid to step up to the microphone and sing, and whenever she did so, she gave it all she had. She charmed her way into the hearts of her listeners.

In February 2000, when the Grammy winners were to be announced, Mom was excited but not overly so. The award was important to her, I'm sure, but I think she felt, in her spirit, that she had already received her reward simply by being recognized and nominated as a solo artist. When her name was called, she was calmly delighted while the rest of her family was over the moon. Interestingly, Dad also won a Grammy the following year for best male country vocal performance for "Solitary Man" from his *American III* album. Though there was, at times, healthy competition between my parents, this was not one of those times. While Mom remained pleased but humble, Dad was exuberant enough for both of them.

In June 2000, we all went back to Virginia and played at the Carter Fold in Hiltons. It was an annual event started by Sara and A.P. Carter's daughter, Janette, and my parents participated whenever they could. That year would be the last time Mom performed there with her full band.

**This signed poster for June Carter Cash's performance
at the Carter Fold hangs in the Cashes' home in Virginia.**

In the house there, a poster, framed and signed by my parents, commemorates the event: Of course, adding Dad's name to the show bill helped the draw, but the fact was, that performance was all about my mother. We got up on that stage at the Carter Fold and gave it all we had, June Carter Cash-style. The crowd danced and sang along, and when we ended the show with "Will the Circle Be Unbroken?" I felt a chill passing through me as I wondered, *Is this the last time we'll sing this song on this stage as a family, with all of us together?* I knew both Mom and Dad were sick, and although they had come back many times when it seemed their diseases had finally gotten the best of them, I knew that strength couldn't last forever. It wasn't that they had ever quit hurting, and that change made their repeated comebacks during those last years possible; it was that they never stopped, no matter what struggles they faced.

Many have asked me, What is the most important lesson your parents taught you? My answer is always the same: persistence. They taught me that lesson in the way they continued their work despite so many obstacles. By the way they lived their lives, they instilled this message in me: In the face of pain, when you are hurting, when all seems against you and you want to give up, persevere. Don't stop. Redouble your efforts. Have faith that God will supply the strength you need to go on. Look to him for your missing pieces, and let him carry you. No matter what stands in your way, always . . .

Press on.

EIGHTEEN

Wildwood Flower

> *June, you are the bright spots.*
> *Love,*
> *John*
>
> A note from June's journal, 1994,
> in John R. Cash's handwriting

My mother built a bridge across the little stream in the backyard of the Virginia home. Once, there was a pond back there, but years ago the area was filled in where the pond had been. Now Maces Stream cuts through the backyard unimpeded, flowing ceaselessly throughout the year. Mom said she built the bridge over the stream "to keep the kids from falling in it," and to build it, she had large logs laid across the stream and planks laid across the logs. Assorted friends and family members helped with the design and construction, and when it was finished, Mom set up a concrete bench near it. She would sit there for hours at a time, watching the water and whistling to the birds.

Across the yard, evergreens planted by Grandpa Eck now press up against the old house, embracing it like the sheltering arms of a loved one. Deer come into the yard at night, feeding on clover and fescue, and wild turkeys gobble eagerly in the spring from within the woods behind. The crickets plead to one another with endless monotony from March through October.

Even in the summer, when daytime temperatures can reach a hundred degrees or higher and the humidity becomes stifling, mornings are almost always cool at the foot of Clinch Mountain. This is only one of the many ways Poor Valley draws us back to her. The verdant hillsides and lush valleys stay within our hearts like youthful nostalgia.

I learned to love this place from my mother, and now I often relate to my own children the tales she passed on to me. And just as I did, my kids listen somewhat distractedly, more concerned with fishing or riding horses or playing with their cousins. But I know these stories will come back to them someday, just as they now come back to me.

Mom told me many times of floating the Holston River in a flat-bottomed boat and using a pole to push the boat over the shallows. Once, she said, an uncle was bitten by an alligator gar while dragging the boat over one particularly shallow section.

"That fish was seven feet long!" Mom told me. "Uncle Bug had to have thirty-one stitches! It's lucky that thing didn't take his leg plum off!"

I've never seen an alligator gar in the Holston, but thanks to that story, I'm always wary of these great fresh-water leviathans when I'm on the water, always careful when wading the river. I pass this folklore on to my children, following my parents' practice of never letting the facts stand in the way of a good story. This tale, however, stands on its own, perhaps proving another thing I remember Mom telling me when I was young: "The truth is almost always stronger and stranger than the best lie, but the truth with a little extra flavor is always tastier."

At the Virginia house I can hear Mom's voice in my memory, calling me to come find her autoharp picks. It is here that I feel her presence most keenly within my heart. Of all her many homes, the house in Maces Springs was the most important to her. It was here in the mountains of Virginia that she could be her uncomplicated and tender self. This was her true home, the place where she and Dad found peace in the last years of their lives.

Everywhere I look, I recall a memory. I see Mom settling in a chair and reaching for her autoharp, wincing a little at the pain of pushing the picks onto her fingertips. Her long fingers had stiffened, like her mother's before her, by arthritis made worse by the constant strumming of musical strings.

She is still in this place, without doubt, resting on one of the porches, talking to the birds, watching her grandchildren, and bidding her loved ones to come, gather around, and sing again the songs of her family. She joins us, I know, when we join hands around the dinner table and pray, offering our thanks to God. She reminds us to come together . . . and to stay together.

In our home back in Hendersonville, Laura and I have a photograph taken by Annie Leibowitz in the front yard of the Virginia house in the summer of 2001. We had been summoned by Dad's creative invitation to celebrate Mom's seventy-second birthday, and the photo captures the images of the happy clan that had gathered: all of Dad's girls, a large number of the grandchildren, Joe and Janette Carter (A.P. and Sara's son and daughter), Flo Wolfe (A.P. and Sara's granddaughter), a few other close cousins who live around Hiltons, Laura (looking beautiful and pregnant, in fact only two weeks from giving birth), my son Joseph, and me. My parents smile happily in the middle of this gathering. It is evident by their proud pose that they are the patriarch and matriarch of this strong-looking and eclectic bunch.

I look at this photo and see the forever-frozen moment of where we all were at that time. For my mother, I now see, this was the last great gathering of the family. She had returned home to Virginia, to the place she had begun, and we were all a part of her. We were her circle.

Sadly, the circle was incomplete and, in some ways, dysfunctional. Mom's own two daughters weren't there for the photo. Carlene was living in Santa Fe at the time and was in the depths of her own addiction. She had

© Annie Leibovitz / Contact Press Images.

**The Carter-Cash family, in Hiltons, Virginia, as captured in 2001
by acclaimed photographer Annie Leibowitz.**

been arrested a number of times for minor criminal offences, had been to treatment centers to no avail, and was on her own path to destruction. Mom called her often, but Carlene seldom answered or returned her calls, and their relationship was at a difficult stage. Carlene had promised to come to Virginia for the family gathering, but she didn't show up.

Mom was saddened by Carlene's absence but kept her spirits high. Her other daughter, Rosey, arrived a few days after the photo was taken, but Rosey was especially hard to be around in those days. Securely held by the clutches of addiction, she had become someone I did not know. The only way to describe her is to say she had become a junky, and true to form, she started causing problems immediately.

Mom wanted Rosey to stay in the house with the rest of the immediate family, but Rosey insisted on staying at a hotel. While Mom was disappointed, I was relieved. During Rosey's two days in Virginia, she seldom came around the home place, which was fortunate, because she didn't get along with my other sisters.

Rosey's appearances at the house were few and brief, but when she came, she stirred things up. I remember her standing inside the house, yelling at Mom with everyone else standing around and listening. We were so shocked, none of us knew what to say or do. Mom absorbed the angry words and, shaken by them, retreated to her room for an hour.

Dad was there and heard the outburst, but he would not confront Rosey or chastise her at all, probably fearing another angry exchange would only hurt Mom more. I'm sure it must have infuriated him, though, to see Mom treated so harshly. But instead of responding to Rosey, he simply followed Mom to her room to comfort her.

Like the rest of us, Dad held inside so many hurtful things . . .

At the Virginia house that week I kept to myself, as I often did when we were there. (And I certainly wanted to stay out of the way of Rosey's bickering with my other sisters.) I had been using drugs and drinking whenever possible before we got there, continuing to live as an addict, lying to and cheating those around me. My predominant behavior at that time ranged somewhere between lost and unpredictable, but amazingly, during that week at the Virginia house, I managed to stay straight, for the most part.

It was my parents' love that had brought us all together. Sick addicts or not, we were a family, one that was much closer than many other families in the entertainment industry.

Overall, our time together that week was fun and easy. We all laughed a lot. At Dad's request, we all prepared a song, poem, or some other gift to perform for Mom. Laura and Rosanne sang the beautiful song "Winding Stream" for her while she relaxed under the old hemlock tree. I sang the Carter Family classic "Worried Man Blues" with my brothers-in-law Jimmy, Fred, and John. Some of the grandchildren wrote poems; others performed new songs they had written especially for the occasion. Except for Rosey's shadowy comings and goings and her memorable outburst, it was a blessed time of laughter and camaraderie. With typical addict paranoia, I had come to the gathering with apprehension, but when the week was over, I left feeling relieved, even jovial.

The float trip on the Holston was unforgettable for all of us; it was then that Mom had been waiting for us at the last bend in the river, wearing her long white dress and broad sunhat, merrily waving her scarf to us as her loved ones floated by.

The week had been one long Carter-Cash clan extravaganza, and when the horde of relatives left, my parents were there alone. I'm sure they slept the whole following week.

The next summer, in 2002, several of us gathered again at the house to make music and to sing praises, both to the Lord above and, this time, to the microphones. Mom had signed a deal with Dualtone Records in Nashville to do a CD entitled *Wildwood Flower*. Appropriately, we were going to record the music at Maces Springs in our Virginia home, gathering in Grandma Maybelle's living room, where the Original Carter Family had rehearsed some seventy years earlier.

I only knew about twenty of the Carter Family's hundreds of songs when Laura and I met, and I'm forever grateful that she pushed me to study their music and learn just what an amazing legacy I'd been given. When I listened to the CDs she shared with me—and as I've listened to their music since—my soul feels as though I've been immersed in the steady roll of the ancient sea. I sense what seems like the inevitable rising of the tide into a shallow bay. At a time when I had emptied myself out, my family's music filled me up.

It was during this time that I began to wake up in many ways. The torrential pain of my youth began to come into focus, and I came to understand and accept that the causes of it were long passed and washed clean. I began to trust God to take care of my parents. And though I would again fall under the control of drugs and alcohol, this was the beginning of my true growing up.

As we prepared to record *Wildwood Flower*, I listened repeatedly to every studio recording the Original Carter Family ever made, well over three hundred songs. This was the music Mom had tried to get me to listen to all my life, but I'd always been too preoccupied with other things to pay sincere attention to it. It had taken another woman I loved, another artist I respected as a fellow musician, to open that world to me.

I am eternally indebted to both Laura and my mother for sparking in me the deep love and appreciation I now have for this music, the deep love and respect I feel for the artistry of my grandmother and my great-aunt and great-uncle. As we worked together, I finally understood the gift my family had left not only to me but to all who cherish the sound and the historical significance of traditional Appalachian music, the soul-stirring music of the mountains. I'm also indebted to my mother for the opportunity she gave me to produce her records—my first professional recorded productions that would launch me into a new musical endeavor I truly enjoy.

I'm also grateful to Laura for helping me realize just who I am as I began to search out and love my musical heritage. Listening to those old Carter Family recordings, I heard songs like "Will You Miss Me When I'm Gone?" and "Sinking in the Lonesome Sea" and "Cannonball Blues." I had discovered my favorite new band. What wonderful music it is.

So we began the *Wildwood Flower* recordings, once again crowding too many people and too much equipment into too little space. Laura and the remarkable Norman Blake would play acoustic guitar. Norman's wife, Nancy, a talented instrumentalist herself, was also a part of the group, and Chuck Turner was the engineer. Barbara Poole played bass, and Dad was in the room for most of the sessions, singing backup and playing guitar. Assorted cousins, grandkids, and friends came and went to lend their voices or musical talents as needed. We set up microphones and just let the machines run, capturing as much of what happened as best as we could.

Mom never stopped, and neither did the loyal Anna Bisceglia. She is mentioned in the *Wildwood Flower* CD's credits; she stood beside Mom constantly as we recorded, constantly waving away the heat with her trusty fan.

We recorded a total of fourteen songs, with at least two versions of each, but Mom never lagged at all; she had the energy of a teenager. She might have been slow to put words together in conversation in-between takes, probably due to the influence of the drugs in her system, but once the music started, the lyrics poured out of her with great spirit and anima-tion, as they'd always done.

She sang most of the words from memory, eyes closed, arms flailing, hands waving above her head to the beat of the song or rhythmically tug-ging at the simple flowered dress covering her knees, as though she wanted to get up and "cut a rug" as she'd done so famously during her Opry and Carter Family days. She sat in her Queen Anne chair and was continuously in motion while performing. Anyone who was there will agree she did as much singing and interpreting of the music with her arms and legs as with her voice. She was a "ball of fire," as she often said. I have never seen any-thing like it. I'm sure it was her unshakable spirit that kept her going.

There were numerous moments of great inspiration during the two days we recorded. Dualtone co-owner Scott Robinson had brought along a small video crew that recorded footage for the four video "enhance-ments" included on the CD. Mom led Scott and the crew around the prop-erty, showing off the bridge over the stream as well as her grape arbor, flowerbeds, and outbuildings. When we weren't recording, Mom was the consummate hostess, making sure everyone had refreshments and a com-fortable place to rest.

One of the most magical moments occurred during the recording of "The Storms Are on the Ocean." Mom wanted to set up mics and record in the yard, but since the forecast warned of rain, we opted for the front porch.

She and Norman recorded the song alone together and the unceasing crickets sang along with them on the original recording. Unfortunately, when the fiddle and cello were overdubbed in the living room a few minutes later, no crickets were recorded on the interior microphones. Too bad.

Looking back now at the videos of that day, I can easily grasp that Mom was sicker than any of us knew at the time. Of course, we all were aware that she was ill, but the reality was, for the last several years she had always seemed to have some sort of infirmity. I, for one, had learned to expect as much out of her when she was ill as when she was not. Mom never failed to push herself to her limits whenever hard work was needed. She was committed, dedicated, and durable, and I had learned not to underestimate her.

Her friend Joyce Trayweek described her then as "a wounded bird, soaring above the clouds. Her wing was broken, but it never stopped her from flying. Her spirit was as true inside as it was when she was sixteen. She had the same heart."

As the late summer heat began to subside at the end of the last day of recording, Mom came to me and said, "Son, thank you for what you did for me. I never could have done it without you." She touched my arm and put her head against my shoulder, as she often did.

I chuckled and shrugged off her thanks. "What did I do, Mom?" I asked. "You're the one who did all the work. All I did was say, 'We're rolling!' every once in a while."

She smiled at me and offered her arm. "Let's go for a walk, son," she said. I helped her down the front steps, and we strolled carefully along the concrete path to the front yard then walked down the drive toward my cousin Joey's house.

"Son," she said, "one day, when you're old, you'll come here and feel the peace of this place. You'll remember being here with me now, and you'll know then what I feel now. You'll miss your loved ones who've gone on—your father and me, perhaps others—and you'll come here to feel closer to them."

We moved on in silence for a moment. She paused, as though hating to say what she wanted to tell me next. "I'll be leaving this world soon to go see the ones I miss," she said. A tear glistened in the corner of her eye.

I had heard her speak this way before, but I had never liked it. "Mom, don't be so sad. You're very much alive right now, and I don't think you'll be leaving anytime in the near future." I stopped and turned to her. "Your light's too bright right now, Mom. You're doing fine," I insisted. "I don't want to hear any more of this."

She smiled patiently, indulgently. "Let's just walk on, son," she said. "I want to show you Grandma's old house."

She led me down the trail to the familiar home I'd visited many times before, but I didn't argue with her. I merely walked by her side, letting her set the pace, listening as she pointed out the features of the beloved place, enjoying the memories she shared.

I left the valley the next day with a new sense of insight into Mom's heart. I had certainly known the facts but had never before felt what I felt then. June Carter Cash was a child of this land, and although she had left it early, whenever she came back here, especially in her later years, she became a child of the land once again. Now I can see that, as much as this land was a part of her, she is a part of the land. I pick up her voice on the wind, hear her laughter in the rustle of the trees, make out her eyes in the summer sky, and I never float the river without remembering her standing there, at the last bend.

Mom departed this world quite a bit sooner than I expected, but in so many ways she is still with me. I still sing with her.

Nineteen

A Tearstained Letter

> *And even if you leave me*
> *I'll be richer when you go.*
> *I'm richer with the lovin' gift you gave me.*
>
> — **Kris Kristofferson**
> "The Loving Gift"
> Recorded by June Carter Cash and
> Johnny Cash, 1972

My parents were as much in love with each other in spring 2003 as they had ever been. Although their love never died during their decades together, there *had* been many times when they had nearly given up on their marriage. Now, however, their relationship was as unbreakable as hardened steel. The fires they had been through had strengthened them to the point that they were truly as one, as much a single being as any two people can be. Most of all, in those last months together, they were the greatest of friends.

Things in my own life were better than they had been for a long time too. I was clean from drugs and alcohol and was consistently attending group meetings. I had accepted my addiction and had been successfully working a recovery program for four months. I had been sober for longer periods, but this time was different. I had finally endured enough pain. I was spending more time with Laura and my children and also more time with my parents. There is no explaining to someone who has never been through it the exact nature of addiction, how reason and logic fail to operate. I had banged my head against the same wall a hundred times, expecting each time to push on through. But something had happened to my spirit in the winter of 2002. I was beginning to see clearly; it was a lesson that was only learned through the cumulative experiences of interior pain. Truly, it was a tremendously difficult education, but I was taking my first steps to becoming a responsible, trustworthy man. I was on a new path to freedom.

While my own health improved, my parents' continued to deteriorate. Dad was now confined to a wheelchair. His legs were swollen, and his skin was fragile and thin so that even the slightest pull could tear off the top layer. He was also prone to falling and did so often. His balance was off, and he simply didn't have any strength. He spent many hours in bed and needed continuous attention.

The women in the house, the ones who had always been Mom's ladies-in-waiting, cared for him day and night. There were also nurses who came regularly every few days. Dad was growing steadily weaker, so it was surprising and inspiring that, despite his infirmity, he was unceasingly productive creatively. He would use all his strength and willpower to make it to the cabin studio across the street. When he couldn't get to the cabin, we brought the studio to him, setting up the microphones and gear in his bedroom or the living room so he could record while sitting in his wheelchair.

His eyesight was also fading, and he could barely read at all anymore. It was a great struggle for him, and about the only way he could make out the words was to use a magnifying projector sent to him by his dear friends Walter and Monica Eschenbach.

In the last year of his life, Dad was reading a book by Gary Jennings called *Aztec*. I don't think he ever finished it, but not because he wasn't enjoying it. He marked throughout his copy, drawing small pictures and underlining passages. He even wrote out quotes from the book and taped them on his desk. But despite the Eschenbachs' gift, Dad became functionally blind toward the end of his life.

Mom and Dad had been sleeping separately for years, with Mom in the master bedroom and Dad on the single bed in his office adjacent to their bedroom and within calling distance. Some may comment that their not sleeping together was an indication that they were no longer together as a couple, but that wasn't the case. It was more of a natural course that evolved out of their consideration for each other. Mom preferred to watch TV late at night with the volume cranked up, and Dad couldn't sleep well with the TV on. Plus, neither of them slept more than a couple hours at a time, and both of them were up frequently through the night. They simply didn't want to disturb each other. They spent many waking hours together watching TV or talking. For the most part, they were only apart during their sleeping hours.

As Dad's condition worsened and it became impossible for him to make it up and down the stairs, he found himself restricted to the third-floor bedrooms, away from the kitchen on the second floor. To solve the problem, they had an elevator installed beginning in the spring of 2003. During the construction, they moved up the hill to what had been the home of Dad's parents, my Grandma Carrie and Grandpa Ray. The house was quite a bit smaller, but it was comfortable and all on one level, so they both found it much easier to get around in.

It was during this time, the next spring after we had started recording Mom's *Wildwood Flower* CD in Virginia, that we returned to the cabin studio to finish the project. Norman and Nancy Blake were there, along with Laura, drummer Rick Lonow, and bass player Dennis Crouch. The creations were as magical as ever. Mom once again rose to the occasion, and we shared many pleasant hours completing the recordings.

The most unforgettable moment and treasured memory came while we were recording "The Heel." We were doing a rather comical version of the song. (This version of "The Heel" was so unusual that upon further consideration we decided not to place it on the *Wildwood Flower* CD. Two years later, however, it was released as a bonus track on the CD *Ring of Fire: The Best of June Carter Cash*.) She was in extraordinary form that day, guiding the session and reciting with great gusto the lyrics for the band. None of us had ever heard the song, or couldn't remember it, and we couldn't find a copy of any of her earlier recordings of it, so we had to guess at the music that accompanied it.

The process was even harder—and funnier—because the song has no melody; it's a poem spoken over background rhythm. What we came up with was a sort of beatnik-Appalachian-jazz kind of thing . . . *wow*. Much of what is heard on the final CD version was put together during the editing process and was built around the bass track (thank you, Dennis) and Mom's vocal. It was a lot of fun, and when I listen to it now, I still see the mischievous gleam in Mom's eyes as she was recording the lyrics that tell of the misdeeds of "that low-down, dirty heel" who treated the girl wrong. The guitar track slides, swells, and fades in a minor key behind her voice, which, when you listen to it, sounds as though she's telling this terrible tale with eyes squinted in rage, lips pursed in tightly controlled anger. I think Mom's acting abilities were coming out in this recording, because it sounds like she was seething with malicious intent . . . I have never seen Mom have so much fun recording. She was in true form.

Mom always had a distinct vision for everything she created, and that was so throughout these days in the studio. Sometimes she seemed distant and would stop making sense when she tried to converse. Then she would surprise me by popping out with some wonderfully original idea or inspired guidance. Unquestionably, the foremost part of my job was simply to make certain the machines were recording at all times to capture everything that happened, and put it all together later.

Since the CD's title was *Wildwood Flower*, Mom wanted the cover to be mostly color photos of her holding fresh flowers, so we set up a photo shoot at the lake house. But although Mom was still beautiful, she also appeared pale and weak. Her spirit didn't shine through as it normally did. In going through the pictures, we came to the conclusion that most of them were unusable, and certainly an album cover shot was not among them.

Another reason why we chose not to use the photos was that by then Mom was quite overweight. She had always loved cheesecake, but in the last two years of her life, she ate more of it than most people eat in a lifetime. More than any other food, she ate cheesecake: cheesecake for breakfast, for lunch, for her afternoon snack, for dinner, and as a bedtime "snack." And when she awoke in the middle of the night, she had another piece.

She would ask any nearby guests or family members, "Honey, would you like a piece of cheesecake?" And if the person answered no, Mom would say, "Oh, just a little piece . . ." as she sliced herself—and the other person—a thick portion. She always put berries on top of it, and, as if it wasn't already sweet enough, she would sprinkle Splenda on top of that pile.

You could find her empty plates everywhere around the house. Even though her cheesecake habit seemed strange, she was actually cute about it. Mom had been thin all her life, but I think during those last two years she may have weighed two hundred pounds. I know that's almost unbelievable to fans who remember her impish form as Little Juney Carter—and her slender and fashionable appearance when she was performing onstage with Dad.

She never had a weight problem until late in her life, but the fact that she did is evident in the videos on her last albums. In those clips she wears full, flowing skirts and long overblouses, and her discomfort shows in the way she fills out her chair and sits with her knees apart. I fear Mom's high-calorie, high-fat diet during that time was a large cause of her heart disease.

So, for at least a couple of reasons, we decided to abandon the idea of using photos on the *Wildwood Flower* cover and opted instead to search out someone who could do a painting for it. The artist I found, Marc Burckhardt, was original and inspired and a pleasure to work with.

My father was also recording during that time, May 2003, for his *American V: A Hundred Highways* CD, but he did most of his sessions in their temporary home. In listening to some of those songs now, especially "Further on Up the Road" and "Why Me?" I hear a sense of urgency and sadness in Dad's voice. Mom stayed in bed during most of Dad's sessions and seldom ventured out. By then she seemed to be constantly going to and from the hospital, and her doctors were urging her to have heart surgery. They wanted to replace a valve and inspect the pacemaker, already installed.

Though I went to see my parents regularly in early May, I felt increasingly unwelcome by some of the household employees. The women who worked for my parents were their caretakers and gave above and beyond the necessary requirements, taking care of Mom and Dad's every need around the clock. Yet they also exerted a sense of control over my parents' lives. It began to feel as if the matriarch and patriarch were not the bosses anymore but that the workers had taken over.

Coming to visit usually meant coming through the gate and then, since the door was usually locked, knocking or ringing the doorbell to be let in. The house is built on a cliff, with a driveway on the bottom level and top. The main door was on the third floor, and the living area on the second. So answering the door required one of the staff members to come up the stairs from the living area on the second floor to let us in.

One staff member, in particular, was known to admonish even family members for "disturbing" Mom or Dad, quickly citing one of many excuses for why it wasn't a good time for anyone to come, even when they had been invited—because Mom and Dad were resting or watching TV or sleeping or bathing or whatever.

Mom always encouraged Laura and me to bring her grandkids by, especially Anna Maybelle. "We'll keep her," she would say. But it became increasingly apparent that most of the household staff, who admittedly, had to do
most of the child tending on the few occasions we did leave Anna Maybelle
there, had a totally opposite attitude about babysitting opportunities.

Even though I tried not to let this increasingly cold attitude get to me,
it sometimes did. The fact was, many family members and even some of
the other employees just stopped coming by altogether.

One day when I went over to spend some time with my parents and to
go over some songs with Dad for his current recording schedule, I pulled in
just in time to see Peggy Knight helping Mom into her Lincoln Town Car.

"Where are you going, Peggy?" I called as our cars met in the driveway.

Rolling down the window and answering without completely stopping
the car, Peggy answered, "I'm taking your mother to the hospital."

I waved to my mother and said, "I'll come see you later, Mom." She fee-
bly smiled back and mouthed the words *I love you* as they pulled away.

I never dreamed it would be the last time she ever spoke to me.

It might seem strange that I didn't immediately turn around and follow
the Town Car to the hospital—or offer to drive Mom there myself. But hos-
pitalizations had become such a commonplace thing for her and Dad at
that time that they had their own suite on the top floor of Baptist Hospital,
and whenever they were admitted, the women on the household staff went
with them. The suite could instantly be transformed into Mom or Dad's
home away from home. Not only were nurses there around the clock,
administering medications, bringing food, and checking vital conditions,
but their employees were there also, doing the same.

Meanwhile, I had learned that the best use of my time was to go to the
parent who was left behind and wait until the other parent had been
admitted and settled into the suite. Then I (or another staff member)
would take the homebound parent to visit the other one.

That day, the doctors went ahead with the heart-valve replacement they'd been wanting to do, and Mom made it through the surgery without incident. Afterward, she was taken to the CCU. Peggy was there when I went to see Mom, and she led me to Mom's bedside.

"I love you, Mom," I said.

Mom was awake. She looked up and smiled at me the best she could, but she couldn't speak due to the oxygen mask covering her face. She reached for my hand and held it tight.

"You're gonna be fine," I told her. "You've got something as good as a brand-new ticker in your chest. You'll be out of here and dancing again in no time."

She did not speak, but her eyes bore into mine, speaking to my heart as clearly as her voice ever had.

No, son, I won't be leaving here alive. I'll be dancing, all right, but not on this earth.

The impact of her unspoken message hit me so hard, I began to lose my balance. I had seen my parents in dire straits so many times before that until that moment this hospital visit seemed like all the others. Now I was feeling something I'd never felt before. I tried to tell myself it was just my imagination.

"You'll be fine," I said, though I didn't believe it.

In response, she smiled again, then closed her eyes.

There were tears in mine as I left.

TWENTY

Oh, Come, Angel Band

My latest sun is sinking fast,
My race is nearly run.
My strongest trials now are past,
My triumph has begun.

—JEFFERSON HASCALL
"Angel Band," 1860

The call came. It was Peggy. I could hear the desperation and sadness in her voice as the words came pouring out, each sentence harder to hear than the last: "Your mother went into cardiac arrest. They got her heart going again, but it was stopped for a long time, over fifteen minutes. She's in a coma. The doctors aren't saying a lot yet, but Dr. Jerkins told me it's likely she'll have severe brain damage if she ever comes out of the coma. Your dad is on the way to the hospital already in the car with Betty [another staff member, Peggy's sister]."

"I'm on my way," was all I could muster.

I quickly got dressed and drove to the hospital. Laura and Anna Maybelle were in Oregon with her family; we had both wanted to be with our mothers on Mother's Day. I called Laura on my way to the hospital.

"I'm coming home," she said.

"No, you stay there. There's nothing you can do here. Take care of Anna Maybelle and stay with your family. I'm okay."

She said again that she wanted to come, but I assured her again that I was fine. I needed her and wanted to bury my face in her hair, cling to her tightly, and release all my anxiety and grief, but I kept that to myself. I was afraid. Certainly Laura could sense this. She came home the next day.

I arrived at Baptist hospital, parked, and hurried to the suite. Betty was there, but Dad had gone to the critical care unit to be with Mom. I hurried to the fifth floor, ran down the hall, and burst into the CCU. A nurse led me into Mom's private room.

She was connected to various machines for life support, her heart rate and other vital signs monitored in endless beeps and drones. She had a tube down her throat and was as still as stone. Dad, beyond distraught, sat beside her in a chair and leaned over her face.

"Baby . . . baby . . . June, I love you. You're gonna be fine. I love you, baby," he said softly, his voice cracking with grief. I came up behind him and softly placed my hands on his shoulders. Peggy was in the room also. I didn't know what to say, but I stood behind him, praying silently.

There was such sadness in Dad's face, such desperation in his eyes, as he begged her gently to come back to him. It was the hardest thing he had experienced since his brother Jack's death in 1944. He rocked gently back and forth, talking to her in fervent tones.

After a while, I went to find the doctor; the report she gave me was bleak. "Your mother flat-lined for almost twenty minutes," she said. "We were able to get her heart beating again, but the possibility of brain damage is considerable. There's no way of knowing to what extent she may have suffered until—and if—she comes out of the coma. We can monitor her brain waves, and when we know something, we'll let you know. Until then, there's nothing to do but wait . . . and keep her on life support."

I was shaken. Devastated. I called all my sisters, one by one, and gave them the news. Most of them said they would come immediately.

When I went back to Mom's room, I found her alone. *Dad must have gone back to the suite to get some rest*, I decided. I sat down beside the bed, my eyes constantly on Mom's face, watching intently for some sign of life, of movement, anything, but she remained still. After thirty minutes or so, Dad returned. I stayed with him a while, then went to the hospital lobby for some coffee.

Afterward I went to the suite and found Dad asleep in a chair. I sat down on the couch, intending to rest my eyes only for a moment, but fell into a deep sleep myself. When I awoke, he was gone again, back to the CCU. I took a sip of cold coffee and followed. Again, I found him leaning over Mom, crying softly to her.

Relating the intensity, the fear, the pain, the monotony, and the worry that filled the next hours . . . and then days . . . is overwhelmingly hard for me, even now, and I struggle through this writing. I remember my sisters arriving, one at a time. Carlene was there, and Rosey, too, a bit more clear-headed than usual and considerably gentler and kinder. Carlene's relationship with Mom had pretty much healed by that time, but I don't know the last time Rosey had seen Mom. They both spent time with her, sitting at her bedside, talking to her soothingly. Cindy, Tara, Kathy, and Rosanne came, too, both to be with Mom and also to support Dad and me. We all did what we could to support each other.

Sometime during the second night, Dad suddenly shouted, "She's waking up!" A laugh rippled through his voice. "She's coming around!"

Mom was moving her head slightly, forward and back or in a faintly detectable rolling motion. Then she opened her eyes; they rolled around in her head, the whites visible, the pupils dilated.

Dad was eager to find hope in the smallest possible gesture. But I put my arm around him, knowing in my heart that Mom wasn't coming back. The doctors said the episode was involuntary movement, and they assured us that her brain-wave scans were grimly conclusive: she was, in essence, brain-dead. Still, Dad prayed for miracles. He begged God to bring her back to him, begged Mom to return. We sat around her bed and prayed with him.

It was becoming increasingly clear that Mom was in some kind of extended limbo. Her heart was still beating strongly, but her mind and spirit had already departed. What we were seeing was simply an empty shell.

Gently, the doctors asked us to consider discontinuing life support. Dad wanted to give her one more day, to see if there were any changes, and the doctors consented.

By the next morning, Mom was still rolling her eyes and opening her mouth, but her condition had worsened. We prayed together, asking God for wisdom to do the right thing. Then, after a brief deliberation, we all agreed that the machines should be turned off.

The room grew suddenly quiet as the nurses flipped off the monitors. I suppose we expected Mom to die immediately, but she didn't. Her pacemaker and new heart valve were working very well, and it kept her body alive.

To someone who has not been through this in life, it may seem unbelievable to pray for your loved one to pass, but as I became increasingly certain that she was already gone, that what I was looking at was merely a shell, and as I watched my father in such pain and grief, I did just that. But death came in God's time, not mine.

The day passed . . . then the night . . . then the next day. Dad's vigil was indescribably arduous and heartbreaking. He went back and forth between the suite and the CCU twenty-four hours a day, usually an hour in each place. We prayed, read Scripture, held hands, and cried.

Four days Mom lived after the life support was turned off. Four days we hovered over her deathbed. And though it was surely the most difficult thing we had ever been through as a family, we all grew closer during her suffering—and ours. Like sheep in the wind, we huddled together in the storm, strengthening each other. All of Mom's closest loved ones were there, and somewhere, somehow, I think she knew.

Laura was by my side as much as she could be; she was with me continually throughout the last day. I held Dad's hand at Mom's bedside as her blood pressure dropped and her heart finally slowed to a stop. My God-brother Ted Rollins read a Bible passage, then we sang "Angel Band" together; it was the song Mom had often said was her favorite:

Oh, bear my longing heart to him who bled and died for me,
Whose blood now cleanses from all sin and gives me victory.
Oh, come, angel band. Come and around me stand.
Oh, bear me away on your snow white wings to my immortal home.
Oh, bear me away on your snow white wings to my immortal home.

On May 15, 2003, June Carter Cash, born Valerie June Carter in Maces Springs, Virginia, went on to join her spirit.

TWENTY-ONE

June Blue

Once again, dear, it's rose time, it's June time.
All the flowers, they bloom as of yore,
And the robin's sweet song is singing
As I walked here to greet you once more.

— A. P. CARTER
"I Found You Among the Roses"
1940

Dad, my sisters, and I sat at a round table in a small room inside the funeral home, making the arrangements. It was a grueling process, a difficult and laborious thing requiring what seemed like a thousand decisions, all made with broken hearts.

Dad wanted Mom's funeral to be open to the general public, and more than that, he wanted to have an open podium time for anyone who loved her to get up and speak. This surprised me, for my father was frail and in his personal life was actually very shy. I was concerned for his health.

"Dad, the funeral could go on for hours," I said.

"Your mother wanted it this way, son."

Dad knew her well. Who was I to argue? She deserved a grand send-off.

Dad also wanted flowers, lots of them. "I want more flowers for her at her funeral than Nashville has ever seen!" he said. It was about then that the funeral director, Tom, asked if we wanted to designate a charity for people to make memorial contributions to in Mom's honor. During the beautiful eulogy she shared at Mom's funeral, my sister Rosanne described what we decided . . . and why:

> She loved flowers and always had them around her. In fact, I don't ever recall seeing her in a room without flowers: not a dressing room, a hotel room, certainly not her home. It seemed as if flowers sprouted wherever she walked. John Carter suggested that the last line of her obituary read: "In lieu of donations, send flowers." We put it in. We thought she would get a kick out of that.

It's not uncommon for memorial services honoring music legends to be held in Ryman Auditorium, the former home of the Grand Ole Opry. But Dad was so feeble and distraught at that point, we knew the longer travel time—it would have meant thirty to forty-five minutes one-way in the car—would be unnecessarily hard on him. So instead the service was held at the nearby First Baptist Church in Hendersonville, a congregation Mom and Dad had sometimes attended. Dad did feel comfortable there. This was the church home of his mother, Carrie, and the pastors were friends with the family.

The building seated approximately two thousand people, and it was nearly full that day, May 18, 2003. As one might expect, the service was filled with music sung by some of music's greatest stars, who were also Mom's intimate friends, including Sheryl Crow, Emmylou Harris, and the Oak Ridge Boys, singing many of Mom's most beloved songs. Laura played "How Great Thou Art" solo on the fiddle, and Janette and Joe Carter performed "Anchored in Love" with Dale Jett. Larry Gatlin and his brothers started the service with what could have been Mom's theme song in perseverance the last few years of her life, "Help Me." It's a prayer that asks, "Lord, help me walk another mile, just one more mile."

Larry, who presided over the service, was one of Mom's "babies." He recalled how she had heard him singing while sitting on a stool at a church thirty years earlier. She wrote his name down on the back of a blank check and bugged Dad repeatedly to listen to him. In this bit of dialogue included in her book, *From the Heart*, Mom jokingly told how she finally took matters in her own hands.

"Who's that playing guitar on my session?"

"That's Larry Gatlin."

"Larry who?"

"From the stool at church. He had to make a car payment. He can sing parts."

"I don't need anyone to sing parts."

"He can write."

"I don't need anyone to write."

"You need someone to write another song for the *Gospel Road* movie. His voice is the voice of an angel, if the angel happens to be a man."[1]

The song Larry wrote for *Gospel Road* was the one he sang in tribute to Mom at her memorial service.

Two pastors preached. Dr. Glenn Weekley, the current senior pastor of First Baptist Church, reminded us that nothing would make Mom happier than to think someone attending her funeral developed a personal relationship with Jesus Christ because of what he or she heard that day. Former pastor Courtney Wilson recalled the day, thirty-six years earlier, when Dad had been four weeks into recovery from "the pills," and Mom called him one Sunday morning and asked if he'd like to go to church with her.

"I don't know," Dad answered. He was still a little shaky about being out in public that early in his recovery.

"We'll come late and sit in the back," Mom answered. And it was then, Pastor Wilson pointed out, that the first miracle might have occurred: "It *is* a miracle if you can come late to a Baptist church and get a seat in the back," he joked.

Pastor Wilson's message that day had been about Jesus Christ, the Living Water, and he noted that Dad recorded the message in a book he wrote eight years later.

Remembering their first encounter all those years ago, he said, "I have to wonder, John, where you would be today if on that Sunday morning June hadn't called and said, 'Let's go to church.' Where would your strength have come from, if not from Jesus Christ?"

He also wondered, he said, how many others Mom had led to the Savior during her life. He called her "the touching hand of God in people's lives."

My sister Rosanne Cash's unforgettable eulogy began by her recalling a day when the telephone rang while she was at Mom's house.

She picked it up and started talking to someone, and after several minutes I wandered off to another room, as it seemed she was deep in conversation. I came back ten or fifteen minutes later, and she was still completely engrossed. I was sitting in the kitchen when she finally hung up a good twenty minutes later. She had a big smile on her face, and she said, "I just had the *nicest* conversation," and she started telling me about this other woman's life, her children, that she had just lost her mother, where she lived, and on and on.

I said, "Well, June, who was it?" and she said, "Why, honey, it was a wrong number." That was June.

In Mom's eyes, there were two kinds of people, Rosanne said: "those she knew and loved, and those she didn't know, and loved. She looked for the best in everyone; it was a way of life for her."

Rosanne grieved not only because June had died but also for "my daddy [who] has lost his dearest companion, his musical counterpart, his soul mate and best friend."

Mom "treated the cashier at the supermarket with the same friendly respect that she treated the president of the United States," Rosanne said, adding,

She was so kind, so charming, and so funny. She made up crazy words that somehow everyone understood. She carried songs in her body the way other people carry red blood cells—she had thousands of them at her immediate disposal; she could recall to the last detail every word and note, and she shared them spontaneously. She loved a particular shade of blue so much that she named it after herself: "June blue."

In recalling her favorite memories of Mom, Rosanne described the week-long birthday celebration at the Virginia house and said that, like the rest of us, she especially loved remembering how, when we were floating the Holston, Mom had waited at the last bend of the river, calling merrily to us and waving her scarf as we floated past. She closed her eulogy with these beautiful words:

So, today, from a bereft husband, seven grieving children, sixteen grandchildren, and three great-grandchildren, we wave to her from *this* shore as she drifts out of our lives. What a legacy she leaves, what a mother she was. I know she has gone ahead of us to the far-side bank. I have faith that when we all round the last bend in the river, she will be standing there on the shore in her big flowered hat and long white skirt, under a June-blue sky, waving her scarf to greet us.

I sat beside my father through the service with my heart full of a thousand thoughts. I was telling Mom good-bye. Through most of the service, my emotions were locked within me, but somewhere toward the end, I felt the tears beginning to well up, as if the flood gates would burst if I didn't let them go. Beside me was the strongest, wisest man I had ever known. When I looked into his eyes, I saw that he was crying. And I joined him.

TWENTY-TWO

A Circle of One

So the Man in Black reached for the sky,
And the bass man lifted him up high,
And God reached down and did His thing,
And the Man in Black took to a wing.

— JUNE CARTER CASH
"Of John"

In the car on the way home from her funeral, Dad turned to me to speak. I saw desperation and deep sadness in his eyes, but also a great determination. "I don't know about you," he said, "but I have to get to work. I have to get into the studio."

"I'm ready, Dad, whatever you want to do," I answered, but without much enthusiasm.

I knew Dad was exhausted from the long ordeal at the hospital and then the funeral, but it seemed that nothing could slow his spirit. I was exhausted, too; I was weak, and I hurt. But as long as Dad had the will to work, I would somehow muster the strength to get back in there and work with him. After all, that's the kind of resolve both my parents had demonstrated for me all their lives. I knew that's what they expected of me, and that's what I expected of myself. I was the son of John R. Cash and June Carter Cash, and I *would* press on.

After the funeral ended that day, a caravan of family cars made its way down the winding Caudill Drive and turned into the driveway at the lake house. We all climbed the hill from the house to the bell garden, a rock and concrete creation George T. Kelly had made years earlier with some thirty brass bells, all painted black. The bells range in size from a small one five inches across to a massive Corps of Engineers bell taken off a bridge on the Tennessee River. Following a long-honored family tradition, we would ring the bells for a loved one who had died.

Dad said a prayer, and we rang the bells seventy-three times, commemorating the years Mom spent in this life. The echoes rang out through the spring day for miles and miles, carried by the wind and the rustling waters of the lake below.

I stayed with Dad a while that day then went home to be with my own family. Cindy, Kathy, Rosanne, and Tara stayed with Dad a while longer. Cindy and Rosanne were there for an extended period.

Dad's utmost pleasure at that point in his life was his books, and being unable to read was a huge loss to him on top of the heartache he felt over Mom's death. He tried to watch a little television now and then but spent most of his time listening to music or sitting quietly, sometimes writing and sometimes simply staring off into who knows where.

In four days, we were back in the studio. We recorded mostly Carter Family songs during the first session. One of the songs Dad chose was the sweet old ballad penned by A.P. Carter, "I Found You Among the Roses," a recording that has never been released. The lyrics must have held eerie and uncanny meaning to him that day:

> Once again, dear, it's rose time,
> It's June time. . . .

I found you among the roses
The day I came back to you.
All my gladness was there in a garden so fair—
Was the happiest moment I knew.[1]

I still don't know how Dad had the strength to sing those words. In fact, I don't know how he had the strength to sing at all, but he did. Such resolve could only have come from God. Without a doubt, Jesus was there with him that day, and all his days, standing by his side. Dad did not lose faith. As he and Mom had always done, he pressed on. And the place where he found the greatest solace was in the studio.

Still, it was apparent to everyone that Dad missed my mother as the body misses lost blood. He could not go on without her for long. Wishing there was something else I could do to help him climb out of the depths of such despair, I spent as much time with him as I was able to do.

"Your mother and I were more in love when she died than we had ever been," he said one day as we sat together in his room. He fumbled for a tissue and his big hand trembled slightly as he roughly wiped his eyes. "I still see her every day. I talk to her all the time."

"Dad," I said, "you and Mom had the greatest human love I have ever seen."

He was constantly distraught, beyond sad; a part of his spirit had died with her. I prayed with him that day and gave him my love. I missed Mom, too, but while I was still able to function, Dad was inconsolable.

The only thing that helped was his music. To combat the grief, he redoubled his creative efforts. He sought out more songs and recorded them day after day. We set up sessions in his round bedroom and also next door at Marty Stuart's house. David Ferguson, Jimmy Tittle, and I were with him for these sessions. Laura would sometimes help, offering her talents as a guitarist, fiddler, and instrument technician. Rick Rubin came to the house for a week. Ostensibly he came to record, but most of all, he was there to be with Dad, his steadfast friend. The two men talked long and often, and Dad seemed to improve while Rick was there.

The other thing Dad did after Mom's funeral was go to work selling or giving away the best part of the furniture and belongings she had accumulated. He seemed determined to remove from the house everything that reminded him of her, though he would barely begin the process before he passed. With his simpler tastes, all of their accumulated possessions weighed heavily upon him with memories of her. Along with this, he was nearly blind, and their shared treasures meant little to him now.

When he decided to clean house, so to speak, Sotheby's international auction house was called in to examine and appraise the various antiques and memorabilia in preparation for an auction, which was eventually held in September 2004. The house buzzed with activity.

Dad still kept on a full household staff, including Peggy, her sisters Shirley and Betty, and Betty's daughter Ramona, as well as Anna Bisceglia and Kti Jensen. Most of his medicines were being administered by these staff members because, for the most part, he was unable to manage them himself.

His diabetes had progressed, and his condition seemed to be steadily deteriorating. He could no longer walk without help, his legs were always swollen, and his eyesight was 95 percent gone. I became concerned that a qualified nurse should be administering his medicines, so I approached Dad about hiring a professional to watch after his medical needs. The loyalty of his staff was not in question to me, though their qualification as medical caregivers was. I simply felt he needed someone with professional training, experience, and expertise to be in charge of these things as his condition worsened.

Although some of the staff resented such changes, I pushed Dad to make them, and today I still stand behind those choices. After some debate, he accepted my suggestions, and a nurse started full time.

Often I have wished that I could have been more helpful and support-ive to Dad during those last months. Our relationship was always close, and while I held no conscious resentments toward him, both of us were a bit guarded about sharing our feelings with each other. In the past I had come to him a few times when I had abused myself to the point of agony. He had prayed with me then and read the Bible to me. He gently assured me that I was safe in the arms of my Creator. We had been through a lot together, both good and bad, but Dad and I did not have the same kind of relationship I'd had with Mom. However, I remembered what he'd done for me, and I did what I could to give back to him.

My sister Cindy came to stay with Dad and helped him sift through Mom's belongings, and I am still grateful for her help. Truly she was the only one at the time who could have done it.

Mom's own daughters weren't able to help with the work. Carlene was not in good shape then, and Rosey was . . . who knows where Rosey was? I was grieving too much to go through Mom's things. I helped some, but there were just too many memories there.

Dad did not sleep in his and my mother's bed after she died; he contin-ued sleeping in the single bed in his office. The room was small but com-fortable, with a few meaningful photos hanging on the walls and the shelves full of books. It was sad for all of us to see him in there, surrounded by the books he loved but was now unable to read. We knew, too, that the photos on the walls were only blurred images to him.

He was in and out of the hospital after Mom died. His body was giving up, but something in him—it had to be his unwavering faith—kept his spirit strong despite the hospital stays, his increasingly serious diabetes-related problems, and his worsening struggles with asthma. He seemed deter-mined to keep on making music as long as there was breath in his body.

Mom and Dad had both understood that this world is only temporary, that the best they could do was to work with their utmost ability to use the talents God had given them, and to love unconditionally those around them. I saw them live this way throughout my life, through the struggles, the addictions, and the sicknesses. I don't think I ever saw them get to a point where they didn't seem to struggle against *something*. Especially in their later years, their lives became a series of challenges, one after the other. But they accepted the difficulties and the pain, and though, like the apostle Paul, they prayed for their problems to be taken away, they also believed that their suffering was not in vain. They demonstrated by the way they worked at the end of their lives that, with God's help, the spirit can grow stronger even as the body gives out.

I was working with some musician friends in the studio the day I got the call that the ambulance was coming to get Dad. He had eaten something that was giving him horrible indigestion, so bad that he was stricken with horrendous pain. Later we learned that his body was producing too much acid and it had entered his bloodstream and was turning his whole system toxic. I got to the lake house just after the paramedics arrived and hurried to find him.

They had him in the master bedroom, the same room where I had sat on Dad's lap as a child and watched cartoons, the same room where Mom had sat, crying, when I had moved out at eighteen. Dad was sitting up on a gurney, wide awake. I saw something in his eyes I had rarely seen before: fear.

"It's gonna be all right, Dad," I told him. I smiled at him and tried to offer an upbeat hand on the shoulder as he was wheeled out to the ambulance, but Dad's eyes told me he didn't believe me. It wasn't gonna be all right, not in the way I meant. I felt the same thing. Even though I had seen him off to the hospital many times before in similar circumstances, I sensed that this would be his last time. His last day. In fact, I felt it with certainty.

I didn't ride in the ambulance but went first to the cabin to let the musicians and the engineer, Chuck Turner, go on home. After I locked up, I went straight to the hospital, where Dad's longtime doctor and friend gave me the prognosis. It wasn't good. "I'm afraid your dad may not make it through this one, John Carter," she said sadly.

Laura met me at the hospital, and Dr. Jerkins asked her to call my sisters on my dad's side and urge them to come straight away. The date was September 11, 2003. Rosanne, in New York, went immediately to the airport and caught a plane. Kathy had already arrived. As fast as they could get there, Tara was coming from Oregon and Cindy from Mississippi, but it was impossible for them to arrive until the next day. I asked a staff member to call Carlene and Rosey, if she could find them.

I stayed with Dad those first few hours in the emergency room then followed when they took him up to the surgical intensive care unit. To tell the truth, I was completely overwhelmed, barely able to function. Over the years I had followed Dad into the hospital repeatedly, and I had seen him at death's door many times, beginning with stomach surgery in 1983, additional abdominal surgery in 1985, heart surgery in 1988, and now whatever illness had befallen him this time. I had seen him defy death over and over again, always winning. I had spent more time with him at hospitals than anyone except my mother and possibly Peggy Knight. This time was different though. I knew, somehow, that the end was coming, and despite his suffering, the thought did not bring me comfort.

Rosanne arrived, and we spent the evening at Dad's bedside. He was awake and somewhat aware but in great pain. Rosanne joined Kathy and me in our vigil. We knew Dad was dying, and so did he. I started to feel that we were draining him in many ways, that our presence was somehow causing him stress. The girls and I had leaned over him for hours, and I thought we needed to give him a break. The truth was, I was nearing my breaking point. I couldn't bear to see Dad suffer.

I left the ICU and went upstairs to a dark, empty room near the suite where we had spent Mom's last days. I sat down on a blue fake-leather chair, and I cried. It seemed to me that Dad—our whole family, actually—

had been surrounded by death for years. It had circled us, threatened us so many times, and just three months earlier, it had claimed a victory. It had taken Mom away from us. I knew in my heart that Dad deserved peace. I knew he was ready to go, to rejoin Mom and meet his Savior face to face. Yet, I prayed for his recovery, for a miracle. And at the same time I prayed, "If he has to go, Lord, please don't let him suffer long, like Mom did."

I didn't intend to fall asleep, but as I sprawled there, weeping and praying, I drifted off. I don't know how long I slept, but the screaming phone awakened me. The doctor's voice was tender but urgent. "John Carter, your dad is leaving us."

The trip down the elevator and through those stark hospital hallways seemed to take forever. I joined Kathy and Rosanne at the bedside. Dad's eyes were shut tight, his breathing labored.

"I love you, Dad," I said, leaning in close. "You've lived the most amazing life, and now you've done enough here. We love you, but you can go on now. You don't have to stay for us. We'll be fine."

Suddenly he blinked and looked up, his eyes wide and seeming to focus on something above him. Immediately I heard a voice within me commanding, *Step back. Your father is going to leave this world now.*

"We have to give him room," I said to Rosanne and Kathy. "We have to step away so he has space to leave."

It probably seemed like a strange thing to say, but they didn't question it. We stepped back from the bed, crying and clinging to each other. The beeping of the monitor slowed then turned into a steady tone. I'm certain I felt a breeze rustle my hair as Dad's spirit passed us, soaring away, bound for peace. When he left that body, he was moving fast.

He had gone on to be with Mom.

Epilogue

The Circle Completed

Maces Springs, Virginia
October 26, 2006

Today is unseasonably cold here at the Virginia house, and the heat is on. I am alone, with the exception of my dog Madison. The October rain washes down Clinch Mountain behind me.

Yesterday, I had dinner with Fern Salyer and her family. My cousins here are real and true—good people. In this place, the world is simpler. I understand how my mother was able to leave these remote mountains, lured away by fame and fortune. I understand her longing to climb the city spires, meet presidents and movie stars, and hear the roar of the crowd beyond the foot lights. But I know, as well, how this place never left her. I know how strongly it pulled her back here. It is the same now for me.

Mom would have been overjoyed to see Reese Witherspoon win an Oscar for portraying the life of June Carter Cash in the acclaimed film *Walk the Line*. But she would be even happier knowing the peace and joy this home brings to my family—my wife, my children, and me, and all the others.

A little over a month after my father passed, I was in Europe when I got the call that Rosey had died. God changed my heart that year of my life, changed it for good. Since the Christmas before Mom died, I have not had a drink or taken any mood-altering drug—nothing, no Tylenol PM or NyQuil, no pain pills or even an Actifed. I'm living one day at a time. I feel free today, as if God has opened my eyes and heart in a way that is liberating and energizing.

I pray to never forget where I have been, never forget how addiction tore through my family like a tornado. My mom's addiction late in life was known to very few people, and I hesitated to write about it now, knowing that if she were here she would likely deny her addiction, as most of us addicts have initially done. But I also know the overriding urge of Mom's heart was to help others. She firmly believed, as I do, that God has the power to bring recovery from addiction. The lessons to be learned from my mother's struggles are great, and I pray I never forget the pain. For I know if I do, I will go back to it.

My mother's heritage is all around me today. I feel it every time I hear "Will the Circle Be Unbroken?" sung during a ceremony at the Country Music Hall of Fame. Though she did not pen the song, I'm sure that through the years she sang it for more audiences than any other twentieth-century entertainer.

And whenever I hear my father's songs from his later career, I sense my mother's spirit supporting him. His voice might be weaker on those recordings that often surprise me now, coming out of a radio somewhere. Yet in his gravely tone I hear hints of a familiar strength arising from within him. I know where that strength came from. I know God's power is behind that voice, but I also hear my mother's inspiration. Even in death she was his sounding board and his foundation.

But for me, Mom's heritage is most vividly apparent in the vivacious personality of Anna Maybelle Cash. We call her Annabelle, and every day I see in her eyes my mother's charm, fire, and love. My five-year-old daughter is already a performer. She seldom stops singing, laughing, and telling silly jokes. I see Mom's energy and beauty in the eyes of my sons Joseph and Jack as well.

Mom's spirit still sparkles within all her grandchildren and great-grand-children, whether related through blood or heart. It's also evident in the hearts of her fans, old and new, the world over. In so many ways, the Wildwood Flower lives on . . .

I hope that someday my own grandchildren and great-grandchildren come back to Maces Springs after I'm gone. I like to picture them sitting on this porch, reading this book, and feeling their grandmother's presence. I hope through these pages they may come to know her in some of the ways I have known her, that though they may read of the pain, they will see the strength and beauty most of all. I pray that they feel the irresistible force of music surging through their hearts and that when they do, they'll know it comes to them through her.

Epigraph, page viii
"Keep on the Sunny Side" by A. P. Carter © 1928, 1962 by Peer International Corporation. Copyright Renewed. International Copyright Secured. Used by permission. All rights reserved.

Prologue: Angel of Appalacia
Epigraph: "You Are My Flower" by A. P. Carter © 1939, 1962, 1964 by Peer International Corporation. Copyright Renewed. International Copyright Secured. Used by permission. All rights reserved.

Chapter 1. The Music of the Mountains
Epigraph: "Homestead on the Farm" by A. P. Carter © 1930 by Peer International Corporation. Copyright Renewed. International Copyright Secured. Used by permission. All rights reserved.

Chapter 2. The World Beyond
1. Taken from *Among My Klediments* by June Carter Cash. Copyright © 1979 by June Carter Cash. Used by permission of Zondervan.
2. Ibid.
3. Ibid.
4. Ibid.
5. Ibid.
6. *Will You Miss Me When I'm Gone?* by Mark Zwonitzer and Charles Hirshberg. Reprinted with the permission of Simon and Schuster Adult Publishing Group (NY: Simon & Schuster, 2004).

Chapter 3. Not Like the Other Girls.
1. Taken from *Among My Klediments* by June Carter Cash. Copyright © 1979 by June Carter Cash. Used by permission of Zondervan.
2. Ibid.

3. *Will You Miss Me When I'm Gone?* by Mark Zwonitzer and Charles Hirshberg. Reprinted with the permission of Simon and Schuster Adult Publishing Group (NY: Simon & Schuster, 2004).

4. June Carter Cash, *Among My Klediments*. Ibid.

5. Ibid.

6. Ibid.

7. Ibid.

8. *From the Heart* by June Carter Cash. Reprinted with the permission of Prentice Hall, an imprint of Simon and Schuster Adult Publishing Group. Copyright 1987 by Prentice-Hall, Inc. All rights reserved.

9. Ibid.

10. June Carter Cash, *Among My Klediments*.

11. Ibid.

12. Ibid.

13. Mark Zwonitzer, *Will You Miss Me When I'm Gone?*

14. June Carter Cash, *Among My Klediments*.

Chapter 4. Opry Star

Epigraph: "Wildwood Flower" by A. P. Carter ©1935 by Peer International Corporation. Copyright Renewed. International Copyright Secured. Used by permission. All rights reserved.

1. *Will You Miss Me When I'm Gone?* by Mark Zwonitzer and Charles Hirshberg. Reprinted with the permission of Simon and Schuster Adult Publishing Group (NY: Simon & Schuster, 2004).

2. Taken from *Among My Klediments* by June Carter Cash. Copyright © 1979 by June Carter Cash. Used by permission of Zondervan.

3. Ibid.

4. Ibid.

5. Ibid.

Chapter 5. When Hearts Like Ours Meet

Epigraph: June Carter and Merle Kilgore, "Ring of Fire." Painted Desert Music Corp. Used by permission. All rights reserved.

1. Steve Turner, *The Man Called Cash* (Nashville: W Publishing Group, a division of Thomas Nelson, 2004). Used by permission. All rights reserved.

2. Ibid.

3. Ibid.

4. Taken from *Among My Klediments* by June Carter Cash. Copyright © 1979 by June Carter Cash. Used by permission of Zondervan.

Chapter 6. Mrs. Johnny Cash

1. Taken from *Among My Klediments* by June Carter Cash. Copyright © 1979 by June Carter Cash. Used by permission of Zondervan.

2. Steve Turner, *The Man Called Cash* (Nashville: W Publishing Group, a division of Thomas Nelson, 2004). Used by permission. All rights reserved.

3. *From the Heart* by June Carter Cash. Reprinted with the permission of Prentice Hall, an imprint of Simon and Schuster. Adult Publishing Group. Copyright 1987 by Prentice-Hall, Inc. All rights reserved.

4. "Flesh and Blood" by Johnny Cash ©1970 Song of Cash, Inc. All rights reserved.

5. "To John" by June Carter Cash ©1975 Song of Cash, Inc. (ASCAP). Administered by Bughouse, a division of Bug Music, Inc. All rights reserved.

Chapter 7. Dreams May Come

Epigraph: Taken from *Among My Klediments* by June Carter Cash. Copyright © 1979 by June Carter Cash. Used by permission of Zondervan.

1. June Carter Cash, *Among My Klediments*. Ibid.

Chapter 8. Hostages

Epigraph: *From the Heart* by June Carter Cash. Reprinted with the permission of Prentice Hall, an imprint of Simon and Schuster. Adult Publishing Group. Copyright 1987 by Prentice-Hall, Inc. All rights reserved.

Chapter 9. Sunday Morning Comin' Down

Epigraph: "Where No One Stands Alone" by Mosie Lister Copyright 1955. Renewed 1983. Mosie Lister Songs (BMI). Administered by The Copyright Company, Nashville, TN. All Rights Reserved. Used By Permission.

Chapter 10. In the Land of the Midnight Sun

Epigraph: *From the Heart* by June Carter Cash. Reprinted with the permission of Prentice Hall, an imprint of Simon and Schuster Adult Publishing Group. Copyright 1987 by Prentice-Hall, Inc. All rights reserved.

1. June Carter Cash, *From the Heart*. Ibid.

Chapter 11. Directions Home

Epigraph: "Lonesome Valley" by A. P. Carter ©1931 by Peer International Corporation. Copyright Renewed. International Copyright Secured. Used by permission. All rights reserved.

Chapter 12. New—and Old—Beginnings

Epigraph: *From the Heart* by June Carter Cash. Reprinted with the permission of Prentice Hall, an imprint of Simon and Schuster Adult Publishing Group. Copyright 1987 by Prentice-Hall, Inc. All rights reserved.

1. Taken from *Among My Klediments* by June Carter Cash. Copyright © 1979 by June Carter Cash. Used by permission of Zondervan.

Chapter 13. Back on the Gospel Road

Epigraph: "Meeting in the Air" by A. P. Carter © by Peer International Corporation. Copyright renewed. International Copyright Secured. Used by permission. All rights reserved.

Chapter 14. The Fall of Camelot

Epigraph: "Wings of Angels" by June Carter Cash. © Song of Cash, Inc. (ASCAP). Administered by Bughouse, a division of Bug Music, Inc. All rights reserved.

Chapter 15. Bear Me Up on Wings of Angels

Epigraph: "Anchored in Love" by A. P. Carter © 1930 by Peer International Corporation. Copyright Renewed. International Copyright Secured. Used by permission. All rights reserved.

Chapter 16. Drawing Pictures in the Sand

Epigraph: "Far Side Banks of Jordan" words by Terry Smith. Published by Silverline Music, Warner/Chappel Music.

1. Terry Smith, "Far Side Banks of Jordan." Ibid.

Chapter 17. First Time to Headline

Epigraph: Taken from *Among My Klediments* by June Carter Cash. Copyright © 1979 by June Carter Cash. Used by permission of Zondervan.

Chapter 19. June Blue

Epigraph: "The Loving Gift" by Kris Kristofferson. © Blackwood Music Inc. EMI. All rights reserved.

Chapter 21. June Blue

Epigraph: "I Found You Among the Roses" by A. P. Carter © (pending) by Peer International Corporation. Copyright Renewed. International Copyright Secured. Used by permission. All rights reserved.

1. *From the Heart* by June Carter Cash. Reprinted with the permission of Prentice Hall, an imprint of Simon and Schuster. Adult Publishing Group. Copyright 1987 by Prentice-Hall, Inc. All rights reserved.

Chapter 22. A Circle of One

Epigraph: "Song to John" by June Carter Cash. © 1980 Song of Cash, Inc. (ASCAP). Administered by Bughouse, a division of Bug, Music Inc. All rights reserved.

1. A. P. Carter, "I Found You Among the Roses" by A. P. Carter © (pending) by Peer International Corporation. Copyright Renewed. International Copyright Secured. Used by permission. All rights reserved.

ANCHORED IN LOVE
A TRIBUTE TO JUNE CARTER CASH

~ ALL NEW RECORDINGS FROM FAMILY AND FRIENDS ~

Sheryl Crow & Willie Nelson

Loretta Lynn

Carlene Carter & Ronnie Dunn

Brad Paisley

Billy Joe Shaver

Dr. Ralph Stanley

Grey De Lisle

Billy Bob Thornton
& The Peasall Sisters

Patty Loveless
& Kris Kristofferson

Rosanne Cash

Elvis Costello

Emmylou Harris

"A GATHERING OF LOVED ONES TO PAY HOMAGE TO HER MUSIC - A LOT OF CREATIVE MAGIC. THIS IS WHAT HAPPENS WHEN YOU PUT GREAT ARTISTS AND GREAT SONGS TOGETHER. IT COMES OUT IN RESPECT TO HER, AND THAT COMMON THREAD IS CLEAR." ~ JOHN CARTER CASH

In Stores Now or Available online.

WWW.DUALTONE.COM **DUALTONE** WWW.ANCHOREDINLOVE.COM